THE TWELVE CHILDREN
OF
CHRISTMAS

WILLIAM CUNNINGHAM
AND
ROBERT CUNNINGHAM

CREATIVE CONTENT CORPORATION
DARIEN, CONNECTICUT

ISBN 978-0-9897695-4-9

eBook ISBN 978-0-9897695-5-6

Cover design: www.ebooklaunch.com

Interior design: www.ebooklaunch.com

For Stacy

Why ...

There were twelve of us—Gale, Janie, Cathy, Kevin, Lynn, Stacy, Bobby, Billy, Debbie, Sean, Danny and Erika—all different and all the same. We were children, the Cunningham kids, together against the world and against the times. The only things we had were each other and hope, endless hope.

We were survivors, the offspring of two alcoholic, self-destructive people, themselves the damaged products of *The Great Depression* and their own warped histories. It's fair to question if we were really even a family, instead of just a band of random children huddled together in a foxhole of time, trying to endure a war raging only around us, the emotional and physical scars now the only things we have in common.

We were never given much religion, although some of us have found it over the years. Hope was our faith and family our church as we struggled to endure a life too harsh. All that seems so long ago now.

But why should that bother any of us, those fading memories? And yet it does, many of us.

Maybe it's because the hope of children never dies. It whispers in your ear, often faint but sometimes clear, to remind you that there is something eternal about a family, something sacred, that must be kept alive, remembered, regardless of the scars.

That's what this book is for—to remember the hope of twelve children, so that their children will remember, and their children.

So, why Christmas memories, in particular? It's definitely not because any of us is gushing with remembrances of idyllic Yuletides past. "I'm not sure I want to go down that rat hole," was one response to the idea of writing *The Twelve Children of Christmas.*

Perhaps it's because Christmas, despite all of its commercially inflated expectations, some of which even managed to seep into our family—despite all that, Christmas crystallized hope for the twelve of us and gave us a vehicle and a time to be a family, to be alive, together and happy, even if only briefly, in the face of our own private war.

Or it could be that voice we all seem to hear every Christmas telling us to remember.

Maybe both, or neither. But twelve children, twelve days of Christmas, twelve stories of hope—the symmetry is natural, maybe even spiritual …

The First Child

FIRST AND LAST

Being the first-born child is supposed to come with certain benefits. Your parents and relatives are supposed to fawn over you like royalty, with every first experience earning you praise and gifts for doing something you were bound to do eventually anyways.

But when you grow up the oldest of twelve children in a poor family with two heavy-drinking, heavy-smoking parents, the benefits are few and short lived. As each new sibling shows up, unexpected and uninvited, you find yourself helping out more and more, trying to be the caring, responsible parent you always wanted your mother and father to be. Your life becomes an endless chorus of "Gale, feed the baby," "Gale, get your sister dressed," "Gale, watch the kids while we go out." Eventually, you realize that even though you're the first born, your life is the last priority.

Few as they may have been, I always try to remember the happy times about being the oldest in my family. Christmas is the most special of those memories for me because I was the one who got to introduce each new sister or brother to the magic of the season.

The first Christmas I really remember was when I was four-years old. I was taking care of Janie on Christmas morning. She was three months old, with big blue eyes and a wide mouth that always seemed to be filled with her plump little fingers. For me, having a baby sister to play with was the best Christmas present ever.

At the time, I was too young to know that Janie was "special." In fact, no one knew Janie had any issues until she was almost two. But it didn't matter because she was always special to me. She was my baby sister, my first sibling, and I loved her.

I don't remember anything I got for Christmas that year, but I do remember playing with Janie a whole lot. I would take an ornament off the Christmas tree and she would grab it. Then we would have a little tug of war—her trying to put it in her mouth and me pulling on it just enough to keep it out. I remember lying on the floor with her by the tree and looking up at the branches and the bright colored lights and the shimmering ornaments. I would reach up and touch the tinsel-covered needles like they were magic while Janie tugged on my shirt sleeve, doing her best to roll over. It was great having someone who adored me.

A year later, I was enjoying another Christmas with another newborn. This time it was my sister Cathy, who was a little over one month old. She was too young to do much except sleep, eat, and cry. Janie and I would put tinsel on our heads and dance around the bassinette, trying to get one of those precious half-smiles that Cathy would grant every now and then.

To my surprise, two years later there was a third sibling celebrating Christmas with us—Kevin, the first boy. He was barely two months old. I was seven, old enough to question where all these babies were coming from and why they always seemed to show up right before Christmas. Janie had arrived in September, Kevin in October, and Cathy in November. Then I realized I was born in October! What was going on here—did babies go on sale in the fall?

Something was up with this trend, but I was too young to figure out what. The whole baby creating process was like a Disney movie to me—the mist cleared, a baby was there and the story started. With this third arrival, I was doing more and more of the feeding, cleaning, and babysitting. This Christmas story was getting old.

But the story seemed to repeat every other year with another surprise baby. Lynn came next, and then Stacy about a year after that. But Stacy was not with us very long. We lost her to SIDS, or "crib death" as it was called back then. She was just four months old. I had been taking care of her since she was born, and I was babysitting her when she died. Nana, my grandmother, was with me. Ma and Dad had gone down to Long Island to visit my aunt.

Even though I was only nine, I felt like a mother who had lost her child. My sense of loss was one of those "firsts" that no kid should ever have to experience. I worried about who was going to introduce Stacy to her first Christmas now. But I couldn't dwell on that during the day because there were still four kids to take care of. At night, though, I would think about Stacy and cry, as softly as I could so that my sisters didn't wake up. Ma was too busy drinking away her own sorrow to console me. I don't remember how Dad handled it. It was hard, but I learned how to comfort myself.

Two years later, Billy and Bobby—the twins, showed up right before Christmas. Two years after that brought Debbie, and then three years later Sean showed up. Now I was the surrogate parent to eight children. It wasn't a Disney movie any more. It was a Charles Dickens novel.

But Disney movies and Dickens novels do have something in common—after struggling for a long time, the main character always manages to find happiness. Just like Disney and Dickens, my struggling life was about to find something special.

It was December 1966, and I had just turned eighteen two months earlier. Things were still tough. Dad and Ma were drinking and smoking more than ever and there still wasn't much money for food or clothes or anything else. But Cathy was helping out more now, and even Lynn too. I had gotten a part-time job after school, and the money from that made things a little easier as well.

We had just moved from the projects in South Boston to our own little house in Tewksbury, a suburb about an hour northwest of Boston. It was a three-bedroom Cape Cod with a small but nice yard. Dad was a Navy veteran of the Korean War and had used the GI Bill to finance it, at least until it was taken away from us a little over a year later. It was a world apart from the roach-infested apartment in Southie. I never expected us to be there very long.

But it wasn't our new home or anything with my family that was making me happy that Christmas season. It was something, or rather, someone, else. His name was Matthew. He was my first real boyfriend, and we were in love.

It was first love—passion and romance and life and death all at once. I was eighteen, he was nineteen, and at that age there is no such thing as a casual relationship. For the first time that I could remember, there was something in my life that was just about me, and I was walking on clouds.

We had met in South Boston and started dating a year earlier, but the spark between us was almost extinguished when I moved to Tewksbury and he enlisted in the Air Force. Given his basic training requirements, it didn't seem like we'd be able to keep seeing each other.

He didn't give up, though. He visited me whenever he was home. We wrote letters to each other and talked on the phone almost every week. When he was home, we'd go to movies, usually the drive-in, for obvious reasons, or travel into Boston, or just walk around the neighborhood talking about topics that only people in love would find interesting.

I wasn't the only one who was happy. My parents, who never had a nice word to say about any young person during the sixties, were taken with Matthew as well. He was taller than average, which Dad liked, probably because he was barely five foot five himself and was always a little self conscious about it. Matthew was on the skinny side and a little mild-mannered, but he was handsome, with an easy smile and a quick laugh. He was also great with kids, which was one of the reasons Ma liked him. He would play kick-the-can and dodge-ball with all my brothers and sisters until I had to pull him away so that we could spend time together.

And on top of all of these wonderful qualities, he could also answer the key question every boyfriend would be asked by my Dad upon meeting him for the first time: *"Do you know who Audie Murphy is?"*

Audie Murphy was a well-known movie actor and, more importantly, the most decorated U.S. combat soldier of World War II, including being awarded the *Congressional Medal of Honor*. He was one of Dad's heroes, and to be worthy of dating his daughter, you had to know who Audie Murphy was. Matthew did know who he was, because I prepped him in advance. I wasn't taking any chances.

With that test passed, Matthew only had to be himself to win over my parents. When he enlisted in the Air Force, he became an All-American icon for them. At times I felt that if they had to choose between the two of us, they would have chosen him. He was my hero as well, and anybody who saw us together could tell we were deeply in love.

Every year, for as long as I could remember, I had been overseeing Christmas for all of my sisters and brothers. I didn't really mind doing it since I loved watching them experience every new Christmas moment, but I had never had any Christmas moments just for myself that I could remember. This year, for the first time, there would be a part of Christmas that was all mine, something special, something just for me. Matthew was coming home for the holidays. It was going to be the best Christmas ever, which wasn't going to be hard since I had never really even had a great one. Still, I could hardly wait. I felt like a kid again.

"What do you mean you're being shipped out?" I said and looked at Matthew with shock and disbelief. "When? Where?"

He had arrived home that morning and taken the train out from Boston to visit me for the afternoon. We had just started our usual walk around the neighborhood when he told me he would be leaving soon for his first deployment.

"Well ... um, it looks like I might be going to Vietnam," Matthew said with a serious look on his face that I had never seen before. "I can't really talk about it much because of military security and all, and I don't know the details yet anyways. All I know is that I'm being trained in navigational support and they suddenly need a lot more of that over in Vietnam. So, they moved up my deployment date. I'll be heading off in a week or two, maybe before Christmas. Definitely before New Year's."

I was devastated. I looked at Matthew, not knowing what to say or how to say it. After I recovered a little, I asked, "Will you be in combat? Fighting?"

"I don't know anything yet. All I know is that my family is freaking out. They're acting like the world is coming to an end. That's one of the reasons I came out here right away. I knew you would be upset too, but at least I can talk to you about it. Every time I look at my mother, she gets tears in her eyes."

Matthew was somber. I knew he wasn't just worried about going to war, but also about what it would do to us.

As my shock wore off, panic seeped in. I followed the news about Vietnam pretty closely. All young people did back then. Everyone knew someone who had been drafted and sent over there. All the news recently was about the increasing number of casualties. And the casualties weren't just ground soldiers anymore. More and more of the reports were about the aerial campaign in Vietnam, including planes being shot down. Matthew wanted to be in the planes.

I knew I had to be strong for Matthew because he needed someone to talk to about this, but as we stood outside my house talking, I could feel the anxiety take hold. My knees started to feel weak. I shifted my feet a little and cleared my throat, trying to shake off the sudden rush of fear.

"What do you want to do?" I asked. "I mean, do you want to talk about it now? Do you want to do something special before Christmas … in case you have to leave early?" I was calming down as I talked. My whole world might be coming to an end, but I was going to make sure Matthew didn't have to worry about me over these last days before he left.

"No, we can talk about it later," he replied, smiling. "Besides, there's not much to talk about. I just want to spend some time with you and not think about it."

I said, "Well, we should plan a special day to celebrate *our* Christmas in case you do have to ship out early. Maybe we could go into Boston and take in the Christmas sights. I have to work on Monday, but we could do it this Tuesday or Wednesday if that works for you?"

I was back to being myself. Yes, it was a crisis for me, but when you grew up like I did, you learned how to handle a crisis. I had a lot of experience making the best out of the worst situation, and this was just about the worst situation I could imagine. I loved Matthew, and I wanted to make it the best Christmas for him that I could. Like so many other Christmases, this one was now going to be about someone else, not me anymore.

We agreed to meet in Boston on Wednesday for our special celebration. Then we spent the rest of the day listening to Christmas songs on the radio, playing with my younger sisters and brothers, and avoiding the topic of Vietnam.

Later that night, as I lay in bed next to my sister Lynn—we all shared beds—I couldn't stop thinking about Matthew going to Vietnam. I thought this must be how girlfriends and wives felt during World War II—constant dread that the person you loved might be killed in a foreign land. I wanted it to be a bad dream that would go away when I woke up, but it was real, and it was terrifying. I wasn't very religious. In fact, I had only been to church a handful of times in my life. But with the prospect of Matthew going to Vietnam, I needed to talk to someone, and God seemed like a good start ... and it was Christmas. I fell asleep that night praying for a miracle.

In 1966, patriotism and anti-war protests collided like the two oceans around Cape Horn. The result was extreme fear and anger on both sides, which too often led to violence. The conservative, older generation warned that the American dream was coming to an end. The liberal, younger generation argued that the military industrial complex was destroying America. Most of us were just confused and afraid. This was a war without a clear enemy or cause.

Fear was now a part of my Christmas. It was like someone had dimmed the lights, and everything was now just a little too dark. Even the good, every day moments—making Christmas decorations with the kids, watching our favorite Christmas specials, listening to Beatles' songs—all seemed less safe and enjoyable. My world that had been so bright and promising was now gray and full of dread. I hadn't lost anything yet, but the fear was getting heavier with each day closer to Matthew's deployment.

That Tuesday, Matthew learned that he would get his orders the week after Christmas. He would be here for Christmas after all, but most likely not New Years. That should have been good news, but it just prolonged the uncertainty for me. I felt incredibly angry. What

WILLIAM AND ROBERT CUNNINGHAM

kind of war-loving, crazy generals would take a soldier away from his loved ones in the middle of the Christmas season? It was just cruel. My happiest Christmas had now become my unhappiest Christmas. The most important person in my life was leaving, possibly forever, and I was helpless to do anything about it.

But I still had him for this Christmas, and I was going to make the most of it. We switched our celebration to the afternoon of Christmas Eve because he was going to be visiting relatives with his family on Christmas Day. We planned to walk around the Boston Common and see the decorations. We were going to do some window shopping at Downtown Crossing too, and maybe visit Jordan Marsh to see Santa's Christmas Village. Then we would have lunch at Hayes & Bickford's, exchange presents, and just be together as long as possible. There would be no talk of war or leaving or anything bad. It was going to be special, because it might have to last us for a very long time, maybe forever.

That Christmas Eve was a typical New England winter day—cold and cloudy with the smell of snow in the air. The temperature was around freezing as I waited for Matthew outside the Park Street subway station on the corner of the Boston Common.

I had dressed up in my nicest holiday outfit—a fitted red, wool sweater with a brown, plaid skirt that ended just above the knees. I wore dark stockings to go with my two-inch black heels. A maroon scarf was wrapped around my long, dark brown hair, which was draped over my black wool coat. I felt like a fashion model, and I was getting a lot of stares from men walking by.

It felt good to be noticed, but the person I really wanted to notice me was almost a half hour late. My wool coat was not nearly as warm as it looked, and I was shivering. Little pellets of icy snow had started to fall. I was getting both anxious and angry that the limited time we had together was going to be cut short by his tardiness. There were no cell phones to call or text each other. I just had to wait for him to show up.

I heard a subway car pull in and pull away. Then a flood of riders came up the stairs and spilled through the open double doorway of the subway entrance. After about thirty seconds, the flood slowed down to a trickle. That's when I saw Matthew bounding up the stairs two at a time, dressed in his full Air Force uniform, carrying his cap in his left hand. He looked so handsome. He smiled and walked over to greet me. I was so excited to see him that I almost forgot how cold and angry I was.

"You look dashing," I said, "but you didn't have to get dressed up in your uniform. Where have you been? My feet are numb and my nose feels like Rudolph's."

"Sorry I'm late. Something came up that I had to take care of," he said as he took my hands and started to rub them to warm me up. "Listen, I have some news to tell you, and I didn't want to tell you it over the phone."

I looked at him with a sudden sense of panic. He hadn't dressed in his uniform for me. He only wore it when he first arrived home or when he was getting ready to leave … The realization suddenly hit me. My chest started to tighten as my breaths came in short gasps.

"Why are you dressed in your uniform?" I asked. "Did they change your orders? Are you leaving today?" Anxiety raced through my body as I looked frantically in his eyes for some reassurance that my fears were just fears.

"Whoa, slow down," Matthew said, smiling and half-laughing as he put his arms around me. "I'm not going anywhere today except around Boston with you. I was just getting my picture taken with my family. My mom wanted to have a family photo with me in my uniform. The photographer was late, so that's why I'm late. I rushed over here and didn't have time to change. And oh, by the way, you look terrific."

"Uh … thank you," I said, a little bewildered. "Is that it? Because you sounded like you had something more important to tell me."

"I do. I have some news about my orders."

Cold air seemed to close in around me as I watched tiny pellets of ice bounce off his uniform. The sounds of the city were suddenly crystal clear. All my senses were heightened as I braced for what he was about to tell me.

"I'm not going to Vietnam, not anytime soon anyways. I'm going to be stationed in New Jersey as part of a support force helping to transport troops overseas. These types of assignments usually last a couple of years. I got the call last night, but I wanted to tell you in person. I do have to leave next week, though. But I'll be back in six weeks for a few days, right before Valentine's Day. I thought—"

I didn't give him a chance to finish. I started kissing and hugging him, making such a scene that people started staring at us.

We spent an amazing day together taking in the Christmas sights of Boston and talking about our future. As we walked through the Public Garden, I said a silent thank you to whatever Christmas spirits were responsible for this wonderful gift. I didn't know what I had done to deserve it, but I was free now of fear and worry, at least for the moment. It felt great.

I think that was the moment when I truly realized that the hardest part of being the oldest in my family was the worry. It was constant. Would there be enough food and clothes for the kids? Would they be safe, healthy? I had never thought about it very much before. Worrying about everyone else was all I knew. Yes, they were my sisters and brothers, and I loved them. It was just the worry never stopped.

But for that Christmas in 1966, everyone I loved was safe, especially Matthew. There was nothing else I wanted. It really was my best Christmas ever.

Matthew and I never did get married. We talked about it, but the timing never seemed right. He never went to Vietnam, but his duties required him to travel more and more, so we saw each other less and less. Then I graduated from high school and moved out to start a new life of my own. We stayed friends after we broke up.

A few years later, I would meet my husband. After we had our first child, I had that same wonderful experience of introducing him to the magic of his first Christmas. As we lay under the tree, looking up through the glittering branches, I remembered that Christmas back in 1966. It reminded me that the first and last most important things about Christmas are the people we love. I remind myself of that every Christmas now.

The Second Child

KEN BERRY
AND THE CHRISTMAS PUPPY

"Janie! Janie! Hurry! It's Ken Berry on the phone!" Kevin shouted to me. "Quick! He's in a rush! He wants to know what you want for Christmas!"

I jumped up from my spot in front of the TV and ran to take the call. *Ken Berry! My all-time favorite actor calling me! I knew this was gonna be the best Christmas ever! Maybe he read my letter and he's gonna invite me to Hollywood to watch him film F-Troop. But I mailed it almost a year ago. Maybe it got lost in the mail or maybe Santa Claus told him to call for my Christmas present! It didn't matter. It was Ken Berry on the phone ... for me!*

I bumped into my sister Lynn and then almost knocked over one of the twins as I ran to the kitchen and grabbed the phone from Kevin.

Lynn yelled, "Watch where you're going!"

I didn't really hear her because I was too excited! I put the phone to my ear and listened for the first words from my idol. After a few seconds of silence that seemed like forever, I realized I had to speak first because he didn't know I was on the phone!

"Hello? Ken Berry? This is Jane Cunningham ... Hello, are you there?" Nobody answered. "Is anybody there?" Still no answer.

"He's not there!" I shouted in a panicked voice. "I think he hung up or we got disconnected!" When I turned to ask Kevin for help, I saw him standing next to the phone with a big, fat grin on his face. His hand was holding down the receiver switch. I started to accuse him of hanging up on Ken Berry, but then he started to laugh like he knew something I didn't.

"Maaaa! Kevin just hung up on Ken Berry before I could talk to him!" I screamed as I tried to stop myself from crying. By this time, Kevin was bent over laughing. Lynn left the kitchen shaking her head. She didn't want to be a part of this argument. The twin I almost knocked over was looking around with a half-smile wondering what was going on. He was eight-years old and I could never tell him apart from his brother.

"What's going on now?" Ma shouted in an irritated voice as she walked in from the porch with a basket of folded laundry.

"Kevin hung up on Ken Berry!" I said, pointing the phone at him.

"Yah! Ken Berry called to tell Janie he was too busy to talk to her!" Kevin replied, still laughing.

"It's a joke, Janie," Ma reassured me. "He's just pulling your leg. Ken Berry didn't call. Don't pay any attention to him." Then she turned to Kevin and said sternly, "You should be ashamed of yourself. You know how much she likes Ken Berry. Say you're sorry."

"I'm sorry," Kevin said but kept chuckling like he didn't really mean it.

Kevin was the oldest of my five brothers. He was twelve and I was fifteen. Like most younger brothers, he thought it was his job to tease his older sister. He teased everybody in the family, not just me. But I always seemed to fall for his jokes more than my other brothers and sisters. My mother told me it was because I was a little gullible. My brothers and sisters sometimes said meaner things. I didn't always understand everything as fast as other kids. But I was smart enough to figure some things out. Right now I had figured out that Kevin was just being a jerk.

"You're a mean jerk!" I yelled at him. "Just wait and see. When I do meet Ken Berry, I'm not going to introduce you to him!"

"Enough already!" Ma said. "Both of you stop arguing. Kevin, go do something. Janie, go back to your TV show, or finish writing your letter to Santa."

Kevin sat down at the kitchen table to continue his homework and I went out to the living room to see if *The Adventures of Superman* was still on. *Rats!* It was over and I missed the ending. In 1967, there were no VCRs or DVRs. If you missed an episode of a show, tough luck. You had to wait until the summer to see it on reruns.

I was angry at Kevin for making me miss the ending, but then I remembered that *F-Troop* was on tomorrow night, and I would get to watch Ken Berry for the first time in three weeks! *F-Troop* was hilarious and Ken Berry was the most handsome actor on TV. I had just joined his fan club and was expecting to get a picture of him in the mail any day. Thinking about him made me happy again.

It was hard not being able to watch my favorite show for so long. The TV we rented had been taken away four weeks ago when we fell behind on the payments. We had pretended we weren't home the first couple of times the man from the rental company came by, but he eventually caught us and we had to let him in to take it. I was sad that day and cried. But Dad got his paycheck yesterday and paid the bill so we could get it back. With Christmas just a few days away, everything was looking up!

I sat down on the couch and leaned on the coffee table to continue writing my Christmas list. I had to finish it by tomorrow for Santa Claus to get it in time to bring my presents. Other kids made fun of me for still believing in him. They said I was too old, but I knew he was real. Just because we didn't get a lot of presents for Christmas didn't mean Santa wasn't real. I always told Ma that Christmas was about family and the Christmas spirit, not presents. She always said I was right.

But I was still hoping for an autographed poster of Ken Berry to hang in my room. So I put it on my list five times to make sure Santa understood this was the one thing I really wanted. I knew he was going to bring it this year. I just knew it.

Then something furry touched my leg. I heard a soft whimpering sound and looked down. It was our dog, Cookie, staring up at me with her big brown eyes like she wanted something. She seemed nervous and nuzzled up against me like she wanted to be petted. So I gave her a hug and told her I would ask Santa to bring her a big, juicy bone for Christmas. She kept acting nervous and pushing up against me, so I began to worry something was wrong. Cookie was a friendly dog but she never asked for this much attention before.

"Maaa!" I yelled towards the kitchen. "Something's wrong with Cookie! She's acting weird. I think she might be sick!"

Kevin shouted back immediately, "She's upset because she just found out they're canceling *F-Troop*!"

I knew he was teasing me again, but that was the last straw for me! I jumped up from the couch, ran into the kitchen and started yelling at him for being a mean jerk again. I said I was going to tear down his sports posters and then made a fist and stuck it close to his face. That got him mad and he started yelling back at me with his own threats. My sister Cathy defended me and told Kevin it was his fault for teasing me. Then Ma started yelling at everyone to be quiet and stop fighting. We kept arguing for another couple of minutes until we all had yelled ourselves out and dinner was ready.

We didn't fight like this every night but we fought often enough. We were a large family, with nine kids and two adults living in a small house in Tewksbury. It was the first and only house we ever owned. All the kids shared two bedrooms, so we spent a lot of time together. Getting on each other's nerves was just something that was bound to happen, every day.

But it seemed like we were arguing more than usual the past couple of weeks. I think it was because things were getting tougher. Dad kept saying there was no money, and we all worried there wouldn't be any presents for Christmas, except the few that Santa always brought. Whatever the reason for all the fighting, I didn't like it, especially since it was Christmas time. After dinner, I looked for Cookie to give her something to eat, but I couldn't find her. I thought she had probably wandered off somewhere to get away from all the yelling.

At last it was Christmas Eve! We had just gotten our Christmas tree and everyone was decorating it. It was a family tradition to get a large, real Christmas tree. The bigger the better. That year was another good one. Dad had waited until the last minute again to buy it so he could get it cheaper. I remember worrying to Ma that we weren't going to have a tree. But Dad had come through.

Decorating the tree was always fun and exciting, even with the arguments over where the lights and ornaments should go. By the end of the night, we had a beautiful tree with lots of tinsel. For the first time in a while, everybody seemed to be in a good mood.

But something was wrong. Nobody remembered seeing Cookie since two days ago when Kevin was teasing me. I said she might have left because of all the yelling, but Dad said she was used to it. Kevin started to say something about Cookie leaving because she didn't like Ken Berry but then he stopped. I think he realized it was Christmas Eve and he should try to be nicer, especially if he wanted that microscope from Santa. But then everyone started talking about what they hoped to find under the tree in the morning and we all forgot about Cookie.

Like most families, Christmas morning came very early in our house. With nine kids sleeping in two rooms across from each other, when one woke up, we all woke up. We all got up at 5:30 and snuck downstairs to peek at the tree with the presents underneath. Then we snuck back upstairs and whispered to each other until we were allowed to go back downstairs for good around seven o'clock.

We all attacked the presents, finding the ones that had our names on them and ripping off the wrapping paper as fast as we could! After ten minutes, all of my presents were opened. I had gotten some things I needed and a couple of things I wanted, but there was nothing with Ken Berry on it. It was a pretty good Christmas. Even though there weren't a lot of presents, there were more than anybody expected. But I was still disappointed. I didn't understand how Santa could forget what I really wanted two years in a row. I asked Ma why Santa didn't bring me the thing I wanted the most. She just said that Santa can't bring everything everybody wants. I believed her but it didn't make me feel any better.

As I looked at my new Beatles album, I thought I heard a whimpering noise. I stopped and listened. I heard it again. Nobody else seemed to hear it. It sounded like Cookie but I couldn't tell where it was coming from. I got up quickly and went over to the front door and opened it. Cookie wasn't there. I looked outside. It was sunny and cold and the yard was covered with trampled snow from last week's storm, but no Cookie.

A rush of cold air came into the room and Dad snapped, "Shut the door! We're not heating the outside. What are you looking for?"

"Is it Ken Barry coming to give you your Christmas present?" Lynn called out. Everybody laughed but I didn't think it was funny.

I said, "I think Cookie's outside. And that's not funny. It's the second year in a row that Santa didn't bring me any Ken Berry things I asked for. Ma, was I bad this year?" I tried to stop myself from crying.

Then I heard it again, a soft whimpering sound. I said, "Shhhh! Hear that, Ma? Everyone listen!" Everybody stopped what they were doing and listened. It was silent.

Ma said, "Janie, I don't hear anything. It's probably just the wind." Everybody went back to talking and looking at each other's presents.

I was sure I heard something. If it was Cookie, I wanted to make sure she was okay. I went to the back porch and opened the door to see if she was there but she wasn't. Then I went to the kitchen and listened. A few seconds later, I heard the soft whimpering again. It was coming from the cellar!

I opened the cellar door and turned on the light. Now I could hear Cookie's whimpering a little louder along with some other strange noises that sounded like chirps. Cookie was in trouble! I needed to find her fast!

I went down the stairs and looked around. Cookie's whimpering was louder and coming from over near the furnace. I walked closer and bent my head around the furnace to see if she was there. It was dark with just a little light coming out of the furnace door from the fire. I blinked my eyes to see better. Then I saw Cookie lying on the floor with her four legs spread out as if she was hurt. She lifted her head when she saw me and whimpered a little louder.

Then I saw them! Four little bundles of fur, squirming next to her tummy, trying to find someplace to feed! Cookie had puppies! On Christmas morning! She had Christmas puppies!

"Maaaa! Everybody! Come quick!" I yelled. "Cookie had puppies!" I ran up the stairs to the kitchen and then into the living room where everyone was. I yelled again, "Cookie had puppies! They're down in the cellar!"

Everyone jumped up and ran to the cellar door. With all the wrapping paper still on the floor, it sounded like a Christmas stampede! Even Dad got up out of his chair. He yelled for everyone to wait for him.

The twins were the fastest to get to the cellar. They didn't wait for Dad. Kevin, Cathy and Lynn were right behind. Then Ma and Dad. Debbie, my six-year old sister, followed and then my oldest sister Gale. She was carrying Sean, who was almost two and the youngest Cunningham at the time. No one waited for me even though I was the one who found Cookie and her puppies.

We all stood or kneeled in a half-circle while Dad and Cathy checked out Cookie and her puppies to make sure they were okay. Cathy was a natural when it came to taking care of animals. She got some food and water for Cookie and talked to her in a soft voice while she picked up and looked at each puppy.

When Cathy finished, she smiled and said, "Two girls, two boys! I think they're all healthy!"

I asked, "Can we keep them?"

Then everyone started to shout and give their opinions. The twins came up with a plan to keep all four puppies. Everybody would get to share a puppy with someone else, except Gale, because she liked cats, not dogs. Sean and Debbie would share one, the twins—Billy and Bobby, Lynn and Kevin, and Cathy and me. That made four. It was a great plan!

"Hold your horses," Dad interrupted. "We're not keeping any of them. We barely have enough food for you kids."

Everyone started to complain and Sean began to cry. Then me too. We all looked at Ma and she looked at Dad.

Dad shook his head and said, "Jesus, Claire." Then he looked at us, grinned and said, "One. That's it. You can vote on which one, but I'm gonna name it."

Everybody started shouting and arguing about which puppy to pick, but nobody could agree. Most of them were talking about the brown one that looked like a little bear cub. I liked the smallest one. He was light and dark brown with a white ring around his neck.

Kevin suddenly stood up and said, "Janie should pick which one we keep. Who knows what would have happened to the puppies if she didn't find them. I bet Santa did it for her instead of getting her Ken Berry stuff."

Cathy added, "I think you're right. Janie, you can name it Ken Berry!" Everybody laughed.

"I agree!" Gale and Lynn said together.

The twins still wanted to keep all four puppies, but they said it was okay with them as long as they could train it. Debbie and Sean were just happy at the idea of a new puppy.

Ma said, "That sounds like a great idea." Now it was a done deal.

I was so excited that I didn't know what to do. Then I started to wonder if it was another one of Kevin's jokes. But when I looked around and saw Ma and everyone smiling, I knew it wasn't. I went over to give Kevin a hug, but twelve-year-old boys don't do hugs.

Kevin stepped behind Gale so I couldn't reach him. He peeked around her and said, "Merry Christmas, Janie, but don't touch me."

Everyone laughed again. Gale put an arm around my shoulder and gave me a big squeeze. It was a special Christmas after all, even without Ken Berry.

Dad said, "Alright, Janie, pick one already."

When I pointed to the one I liked, Cathy picked him up and handed him to me to hold. He nuzzled up against my neck. Everybody clapped!

It took Dad a few days to think of a name. When I asked if we could name him *Ken Berry*, Dad said it wasn't a good idea to name a pet after someone you liked because you could be stuck with the name even if you stopped liking them. He grinned and pointed to a tattoo of Ma's name on his arm and said, "See?"

Ma was standing there but I don't think she thought it was funny.

Dad finally picked the name of a dog from a song he sang when he was a boy, *Rattler*. So that's what we started calling our new puppy. It wasn't as good as *Ken Berry*, but I still liked it.

Whenever I think about my favorite Christmas, I remember that one when Rattler was born and how Kevin made it special for me. He didn't stop teasing me and everyone else until he got older, but we got along better after that. The next Christmas, he even gave me a Ken Berry poster. It was the best present I got that year.

Last week was my birthday. My family threw me a big party because it was a big birthday, but I'm not going to say which one. Kevin gave me my favorite present again, a 32-inch HD television for my bedroom. He also bought me the complete *F-Troop* DVD set. I'm going to make some popcorn and he's going to come over with some of my other brothers and sisters to watch our favorite episodes. I'll see if Ken Berry still looks as handsome as I remember.

The Third Child

THE SPARKLE OF HOPE

My first Christmas as a Cunningham was in 1953. I was thirty-nine days old, but I don't remember that one, of course. I was the third child and the third girl—Catherine, with a "C", not a "K". I spent the next seventeen Christmases at home with my parents and siblings.

My last Christmas as a Cunningham, at least the first time around, was in 1970. I was seventeen and a senior in high school. I don't remember that Christmas either.

I got married the following summer after graduating, had two children before I was twenty, and got divorced twenty years later. Now I'm a Cunningham again. Actually, I was still a Cunningham even when I was married. Once a Cunningham, always a Cunningham.

I do remember that eleven of us had been born by the time of my last Christmas at home, five boys and six girls, but only ten of us were alive. My sister Stacy, the sixth child, had died at four months old. As for the Christmases in between those first and last ones, I only have scattered memories, but not because I'm fifty-nine years old now. It's because they were all blurs to me, even while I was living them.

The Christmas after Stacy died is the first one I sort of remember. Everyone was sad, especially Ma. I was only five, but I remember feeling bad for her and guilty about wanting this new doll. Ma said that I should be thinking about my little sister more than presents for myself. So, I wished for Santa to give God a new doll to give to Stacy too. When it wasn't under the tree that Christmas morning, I convinced myself that Stacy had a new doll in Heaven. It made me feel better, but I still recall being disappointed and wondering why Santa couldn't give us each one. I guess that doesn't really count as a special Christmas memory.

Probably the Christmas that sticks out most in my memory is when I was eight. It was 1961, and we had just moved into the Old Colony Housing Project in South Boston. It was considered one of Boston's slums even then. The truth is I have some good memories from growing up there. We had been living in Roxbury before that, which was worse. It was the fifth time I had moved. I was always good at math.

At least our apartment was big, with four bedrooms, which we needed because there were eight kids by then, plus Ma and Dad. The youngest one that Christmas was Debbie. She had just been born a few months earlier and was in a crib in Ma and Dad's room. Kevin, the oldest boy, shared a bedroom with Billy and Bobby, the twins, who were only two. Gale and Janie, the two oldest, were in one bedroom, and Lynn and I shared the other. It was a pretty good setup, and the cockroaches weren't nearly as bad as in Roxbury.

That Christmas was when I first learned about *Globe Santa*, the charity service run by The Boston Globe. It gives Christmas presents to the children of families in need. Back then, you had to send a letter to *Globe Santa* telling your story and explaining why you needed assistance, as well as providing information on your children under twelve years old to make sure appropriate gifts were delivered if you were approved.

I remember it was a cold December afternoon when Ma took me and Janie for a walk to buy a stamp and mail the letter. Gale stayed at home to watch the other kids. Ma took Janie because she was acting up, and Gale didn't know how to handle her. Janie was "special," but she was smart in many ways and knew how to manipulate situations to get her way, especially when it came to Ma.

Ma took me along because she needed someone to find cigarette butts that were long enough to still smoke. We used to do that all the time for her and Dad when they didn't have enough money to buy new cigarettes. I think Ma knew I was the best at finding the longest ones. My secret was to check along the curb by the bus stops. That was where people would flick their used cigarettes on the sidewalk or in the street just before getting on the bus. I'd often find a nearly whole cigarette, uncrushed, sitting in the crevice where the curb met the street. Those were keepers.

I remember us kids going for walks at night in South Boston with either Ma or Dad, sometimes both. Gale, Kevin, Lynn and I would compete to see who could find the most usable cigarette butts. Janie would try to compete too, but she wasn't very good because of her bad eyesight. Ma would tell us if one was a keeper or had to be thrown away, sort of like Dad did when he took us fishing and we caught a small flounder or cod. We'd count the butts that were keepers and declare who was the winner when we got back to our apartment. If Kevin was losing, he would always try to cheat. He was so competitive. We had a lot of fun with that game.

Anyway, back to that Christmas. The wind was really biting that day as Ma, Janie and I made our way to the corner store a few blocks down on East 8th Street. Ma used a nickel to buy a four cent stamp and let Janie and I buy two pieces of candy with the remaining penny. That memory is so clear because it was the first time I ever went in that store. I was amazed at how much candy and cool stuff there was. It's the store where Gale, Janie and I would buy all of our Beatles cards a few years later when they became such a hit in the U.S. It's funny how that store has stuck in my memory all these years.

After Ma mailed her letter, she lit up one of the long cigarette butts I had found, and we headed back in the bitter cold and wind to our apartment. I asked her who the letter was to, and she told me *Globe Santa*. When I asked her who that was, Janie interrupted and answered that Dad said it was the Santa Claus for poor people. I insisted there was only one Santa Claus and that he was for everyone. Ma told Janie that Dad was just teasing her.

Then Ma explained to me that *Globe Santa* was the people who kept track of families who had moved so that Santa Claus could make sure they got their presents. It was an explanation I happily accepted since I had been worrying if Santa would know where we had just moved to. I had convinced myself that moving so much was why we never got many gifts at Christmas time. Now that I knew about *Globe*

Santa, I wondered why Ma hadn't sent a letter to them all the other times we had moved.

That was the year that I had been collecting cardboard license plates from cereal boxes with the names of each state on them. I was obsessed with geography, especially the fifty states, and had asked for a bunch of geography related things on my Christmas list to Santa. I still love geography to this day.

That was also the year that Ma worked at Bradford Novelty making Christmas ornaments. I remember she brought a box of rejected ones home for us to decorate the tree with. They were gleaming silver and gold, filled with different colored angel hair, in all shapes and sizes. When the tree lights were on—the big, multi-colored, painted ones from back then—you could see sparkling reflections everywhere. I remember thinking we had the best decorated tree ever. I just loved that tree.

To this day, I love anything that sparkles—icicles after a freezing snow storm, the reflection of the sun on the ocean, dew on the grass in the morning light, and, of course, greeting cards with glitter. They're a must every Christmas.

I remember it was the afternoon of Christmas Eve, and all of us kids were making different decorations to hang up. I had just learned how to make snowflakes in school and was teaching Janie and Kevin when someone knocked on our apartment door. Ma went and opened it.

A tall man was standing in the hallway in a Santa hat holding two big brown paper bags filled with what looked like toys. Ma exclaimed something and smiled. Then I heard her say to him that she didn't think she was getting anything since she hadn't heard from them. I didn't know who the man was or what Ma was talking about. The man replied that our phone was out of service when they tried to call and the letter they sent was probably delayed in the mail. Ma then turned around and told all of us to go to her bedroom for a few minutes while she talked to the man.

Once in Ma and Dad's bedroom, Janie started to get worked up and asked Gale if that was the man from *Globe Santa*. I said it couldn't be because *Globe Santa* was just for letting Santa know where we had moved to so he could bring us our presents. But Gale said it was the *Globe Santa* man. That didn't make any sense to me.

I asked Gale why the *Globe Santa* man was bringing our presents from Santa early. Kevin and Lynn listened closely to our discussion. Gale explained that *Globe Santa* brought extra presents to families who had a lot of kids but not a lot of money. She said we should be excited because we were going to get even more presents this year.

I was still confused. When I heard the front door close, I ran out to the kitchen and asked Ma if the man was from *Globe Santa*. She said he was, so I asked why he had brought us toys if he had already told Santa where we had moved to. Ma smiled and said that *Globe Santa* also gave extra toys to families with a lot of young children, the same thing Gale had told me, except Ma didn't say it was because we were poor. I remember she seemed relieved.

Since it was Christmas Eve, Dad got home from work early and proceeded to sit down in the kitchen to have a few beers while he listened to Elvis Pressley sing Christmas songs on the radio. I remember Janie suddenly screaming a bit dramatically when a cockroach raced across the kitchen floor because Ma had moved some pans under the sink while she made dinner. Kevin ran to try to step on it, but Dad told him it might be their Santa and none of the little roaches would end up getting any presents if he killed it. Kevin paused and looked at Dad, who smiled and laughed. Kevin realized he was joking, but it was too late. Santa Roach had escaped. Dad was funny when he was only a little drunk.

Then Ma chimed in and said the roach looked more like Rudolph. Gale added something about eight cockroaches pulling a sleigh full of crumbs, and everyone laughed. I thought it was disgusting, but it became a running joke in our family every Christmas after that. I could never get the image out of my head.

Gale sang all of us Christmas carols before we fell asleep. I remember waking up later on and hearing Ma and Dad arguing. I went out to see what was going on. They were sitting at the kitchen table smoking, with a glass of beer in front of each of them. Some of the toys from the Globe Santa man were on the table. I could tell Ma was in the middle of wrapping them. Dad said Santa hadn't come yet, so I'd better get back in bed. Ma asked if I had a bad dream. I said no, and she told me to go back to bed too.

I fell back to sleep right away but woke up again later on. It was quiet this time. I snuck out to the front room and looked to see if Santa had come. All the lights were off, and Ma and Dad were in bed. I crept closer and peeked around my father's old lounge chair. I remember the ornaments and tinsel on the tree sparkling in the dark from the street light glowing through the window of our apartment. There were presents too. I couldn't tell how many, but there were more than I had ever seen before. It was magical.

The twins woke all of us up early that Christmas morning. Dad must have been a little hung over because he snapped at us from his bed when we peeked in to ask Ma if we could open the presents. She lifted her head and said she would be out in a few minutes. Then she told Gale to give Debbie a bottle and promptly fell back to sleep.

We all huddled on the floor where the hallway opened to the front room, right next to the radiator so we could keep warm. We tried to guess which presents belonged to each of us while we waited for Ma to get up. I remember it being cold and pulling my knees up to my chin to stay warm as I marveled at our tree sparkling in the morning sunlight seeping into our apartment.

When Ma finally came out of her bedroom, we had to wait to open our presents while she smoked a cigarette. Then she and Gale handed out our presents. There didn't seem to be as many as I thought when I snuck out to peek at the tree, and they all said "From Santa."

The last present Ma handed to me was a big, nicely wrapped box that made a funny noise when I shook it. I ripped off the wrapping paper and saw that it was a giant jigsaw puzzle of the United States. I recognized the box from one of the bags of presents the man from Globe Santa was holding. I loved it and thought the person who picked it out for me really knew me. I felt so special that someone other than Santa actually cared enough to get me what I wanted.

As I sat there staring at my puzzle, I suddenly wondered why all the gifts said "From Santa" when a lot of them had come from the Globe Santa man. That's when I noticed it was Ma's writing on all of my presents, and everyone else's too. I knew it was hers because she had really nice hand writing. I remember how she always made a big deal over penmanship.

Anyway, that's when I realized that none of our presents had really come from Santa. At first, I thought maybe Santa had missed us because we had moved again and Ma was just covering for him. But I knew that didn't make sense because that's what Globe Santa was supposedly for. It was the first time I thought that Santa Claus might not be real. That was hard.

No one else seemed to get what they really wanted that year except me. The younger kids didn't know what to think, but the older ones all seemed disappointed. I remember Ma looking sad that Christmas morning. I felt guilty, as if it was my fault that I was the only one who had gotten what I asked for. I know now that I was just lucky to get what I wanted. It was the first time I truly understood that Christmas wasn't all sparkle.

After that Christmas, I don't really have any strong, distinct memories, probably because it was the same story every year—feeling bad for my mother because she could never afford enough presents for all of us and feeling guilty for wanting things that Ma and Dad could never give us. I do remember that Globe Santa became kind of a tradition from that Christmas on, although Ma neglected to get around to signing up for it some years.

The irony is that we really weren't poor enough to qualify for *Globe Santa* because Dad actually brought home a decent week's pay as a truck driver. The problem was that it wasn't close to enough when you factored in eight or nine kids living at home during any given Christmas, especially given the money spent on beer and cigarettes, although the *Globe Santa* man never knew about that. I'm sure Ma just lied about what Dad really made.

After I got married and had my own children, I was determined that they would remember their Christmases and never feel guilty about wanting presents. Guilt was a gift I never wanted waiting for them under the tree like it had been every Christmas for me.

Instead, I wanted to give my children the same sparkle of lights, tinsel, and silver and gold ornaments I looked so forward to every year—that sparkle of hope that hung on the tree every Christmas morning for my brothers and sisters and me. It's what held us together through all those Christmases, despite the disappointments. Now that I've written this, I realize it even gave us a cherished memory here and there.

I believe with all my heart that the sparkle of hope is the most precious gift we can give our children. I know it's hard to believe, but somehow, and I don't know how, that present was under the tree waiting for me every Christmas growing up. Maybe there really is a Santa Claus.

The Fourth Child

A .22 CALIBER CHRISTMAS

If I'm going to be honest, I really don't have any good Christmas memories growing up. There were memorable Christmases, but none of them were good, at least in a traditional sense.

I was the first boy in my family—in a way, the first son of Christmas. That made me special, particularly with Dad, but Ma too. I think that bothered my older sisters and Lynn, who was a year and a half younger than me. It's not that I got more presents than them, because I didn't. I remember since there were never very many for any of us on Christmas morning. But I think it might have seemed like I did because Dad and Ma made a bigger deal out of what I got, even if it wasn't much.

When I think about it, the Christmas that comes to mind first was one on Bennett Street in Beverly. I was thirteen. We lived in a three bedroom apartment on the first floor of a triple-decker, which was New England's version of a tenement building back then.

We had moved there a little over a year earlier after losing the small Cape Cod that Dad and Ma had bought in Tewksbury, the only place we ever lived that was ours. It wasn't ours for long. Just a year and a half and one Christmas. And I think the lights and heat were turned off during that one because the bills hadn't been paid. That's a Christmas I don't care to remember.

Back to Bennett Street. I remember Ma was pregnant with Danny, so she wasn't drinking very much, which meant Dad was more under control as well. Gale, the oldest, had already moved out on her own. That left eight kids plus Rattler, our dog, and Spooky, the emaciated dark gray cat that Billy and Bobby, my nine-year-old twin brothers, had found and brought home. Everything seemed relatively stable after moving twice in three years. It felt like it was going to be a good Christmas, a trap I seemed to fall into every year.

Pan to the afternoon of Christmas Eve. We're all in the apartment waiting for Dad to get home so Ma could do some last minute Christmas shopping and buy a turkey for Christmas dinner. Dad was a truck driver and had the day off from work, but he had gone in to pick up his paycheck. He was supposed to be home around noon. It was almost four o'clock. Ma was snapping at everyone because she was worried that Dad wouldn't get home in time to get to the stores before they closed. That would mean spaghetti for Christmas, with ketchup.

The older kids like me were all anxious, feeding off of Ma. The younger ones were feeding off the older ones and were anxious too. They had sensed something was wrong, but they didn't know what.

To keep busy while we waited for Dad, we made multi-colored Christmas rings out of construction paper and hung them around the doorways. Then Cathy, who was two years older than me, taught all of us how to cut snowflakes out of notebook paper. She did it every year, because we forget how to do it every year. We taped them to the windows and pretended it was snowing outside. They were pretty cool. Actually, that's sort of a good memory.

But that was enough family nice time for the eight of us. Before long, everyone started arguing and fighting over nothing. Cathy was crying about something Ma had said to her, while Janie was trying to provoke Lynn to get Ma's attention. Debbie was annoying Billy and Bobby over something, knowing I would step in to defend her. I always took sides against the twins for some reason. They were the only boys close to my age. Sean was only three. I had started to take his side against them too. It was instinctive at the time.

"Bah humbug, Pilgrim," a voice suddenly slurred loudly from the front door in the hallway. Dad was home, and he was doing his impersonation of John Wayne playing Scrooge. That meant he was drunk.

Dad was sort of insecure when he was sober, even self-conscious, but after a few beers, he could be pretty funny. He was a small man, but he had a big voice when he drank, and he loved John Wayne. His impersonation was pretty bad, but I remember having a lot of fun with it.

Everyone scrambled to greet Dad in the hallway that ran from the front door to the kitchen. He was a little surprised since we barely acknowledged him most of the time when he got home from work. But today, the older kids knew he was the key to whether we had a decent or lousy Christmas because he had the money Ma needed to buy last minute presents and food. And the younger ones were following the older ones.

Dad finally getting home was a relief for everyone, but I knew it was temporary since there was always a cloud of worry about something hanging over us, like the residual smoke from Ma and Dad's cigarettes that never seemed to go away. The anxiety and smoke are what I remember most about growing up, even more than the beer, because they were constant.

"Jesus Christ, Bob," Ma snapped at him. "Where have you been? I'm never going to make it to the stores before they close."

"There you go again, Claire," Dad replied, weaving down the hallway towards the kitchen. "I walk in the door and the first thing you do is give me a hard time. I guess you don't want this turkey then."

"Ma, he has a turkey," Janie shouted.

"Dad, where'd the turkey come from?" I asked.

"Where in the blazes did you get that?" Ma asked, standing at the entrance to the kitchen.

"Turkey, turkey … It's a turkey! I wanna see!" Sean exclaimed.

"Did someone say we got a turkey?" Cathy asked, walking into the kitchen.

Dad plopped the huge thing on the kitchen table, and everyone circled it. It was like something out of *A Christmas Carol,* but unfortunately real.

"I hit it with my car," Dad said and smirked. "It was trying to cross the road to the get to the other side."

"He did not, did he Ma?" Janie said, not realizing Dad was joking.

"No, of course not," Ma said to Janie and then glared at Dad. "I still have to get to the grocery store before it closes. And I still need to do some Christmas shopping too. You're drunk as a skunk. How am I going to get there?"

For some reason, Ma never learned how to drive. I guess being able to drive would have made it harder to feign helplessness.

"I had a couple of beers for cryin' out loud," Dad said and put a brown paper grocery bag with four quarts of Pabst Blue Ribbon on the kitchen table next to the turkey. He plopped down in a chair and took out a cigarette.

"A couple, my eye," Ma said and sat down slowly at the table, favoring her pregnant stomach. Then she pointed at the turkey and asked, "So where did that really come from?"

"The owners at work bought a bunch of turkeys and food to give to anyone who needed it," Dad answered. "I got the biggest one when I told them I had nine kids at home. There's a bag of food in my car too. Billy or Bobby, go bring it in."

Because Dad could never tell my twin brothers apart, he always called them "Billy or Bobby", even when he was talking to just one of them. They both raced down the hallway and out of the apartment, with Debbie following close behind.

I leaned on the kitchen table and said, "Dad, we only have eight kids."

"There'll be nine pretty soon," Dad replied, then grinned and pointed at Ma's stomach. "Lynn, put these beers in the refrigerator. And open one up for me … and get me a glass."

Lynn begrudgingly did what he asked. Dad almost never asked me to open his beers or make him coffee in the morning. He usually told one of the girls and sometimes Billy or Bobby.

When Billy and Bobby brought in the bag of food, Ma looked inside and said, "Oh, this is great, almost everything I needed. I can just send Cathy to A&P for a few things."

Ma got up, grabbed a glass and poured a little beer from Dad's bottle into it. She lit up a cigarette and sat down slowly again. She seemed relieved.

I walked over to Ma and whispered, "What about Christmas shopping?"

"I'm just taking a break," she said. "Don't worry. It's only five o'clock. The stores are open until eight."

At six o'clock, Dad was listening to Elvis Presley singing Christmas songs on the radio while Ma sipped her beer and smoked another cigarette. All of us kids were doing different things around the apartment, waiting anxiously to see if Ma would get money from Dad to go Christmas shopping. It was worse than waiting for Santa.

Suddenly, Janie came rushing into the kitchen in a panic and yelled, "Cathy says the stores close at seven o'clock! It's too late to go Christmas shopping. We're not going to get any Christmas presents, besides the ones from Santa. It's Dad's fault."

Janie was the second oldest after Gale. She had special needs, and Ma treated her like she had to be protected all the time. But Janie was smart in her own way, and she used her intelligence to manipulate situations when she was feeling anxious or wanted Ma's attention.

That night, it was both. Janie's target to get Ma's attention was Dad. It was easy since he was drunk. Besides her panic tantrum, Janie faked several violent gestures as if she was going to hit Dad. It was always the same routine. Dad would try to ignore Janie but eventually get angry and lashed out verbally at her. Ma always sat by, watching the show like she had orchestrated it, usually half drunk herself.

Tonight, though, Janie got Ma going as well because the stores really were closing at seven and not eight. Ma started to panic and said to Dad, "I need some money or else the kids won't have anything under the tree."

Janie started to rant again, which got Dad to yell at Ma, "Will you get her out of the kitchen, Claire, or no one's going to get any presents!"

"Janie, go to your room and calm down!" Ma shouted, then looked at Dad and said, "I need some money. You cashed your check didn't you?"

"I had to pay back money I borrowed from some guys. I don't have any to give you," Dad said and turned the radio up to drown out Janie's crying from the hallway.

"You have money, and I need some," Ma snapped at him, then got up and stormed out of the kitchen towards the bathroom.

I stood in the entrance from the front room to the kitchen listening to everything. Billy and Bobby had taken Debbie and Sean over by the Christmas tree to sing songs and distract them. Lynn and Cathy were in their room talking or doing something to block everything out. And of course, Janie had followed Ma to the bathroom and stood outside the door crying.

I walked over to Dad and asked, "Are you really not going to give Ma any money for Christmas presents?"

He looked at me and turned down the radio. Then he flicked some ashes from his cigarette into the ashtray and said, "You gotta speak up, Kevin. I don't hear well in that ear."

"Are you really not going to give Ma any money for presents?" I repeated.

"She doesn't need any money. Santa brings all the presents," he answered and looked away.

Dad was usually pretty cheerful when he drank, but sometimes he was mischievous, even nasty. I could tell he was all three tonight since he was avoiding making eye contact.

I said, "I'm thirteen and there's no such thing as Santa. If you don't give Ma some money, no one's going to get anything for Christmas."

"I gave her money for presents last week. I don't know what she did with it," Dad replied.

I remember starting to tear up a little and saying, "It doesn't matter, Dad. You're the father. You're supposed to make sure we get presents."

Dad glanced at me, a look of guilt on his face, but then his eyes seemed to turn angry. He looked away and snapped, "Go get the 22 out of my closet."

I hesitated but then hurried to Dad's bedroom closet where he kept his .22 caliber rifle. Dad had taught me how to shoot it a few years earlier, but he'd only taken me to practice a couple of times. I sometimes snuck it out and pretended I was shooting at things from the back porch.

"Why do you want it," I asked defiantly as I stood in the kitchen holding the rifle. I was pretty nervous.

"Just put it on the table, Kevin," Dad said.

I placed the rifle on the table and stood there waiting while Dad listened to some country and western Christmas music. He glanced at me and smiled a few times, ignoring the rifle.

Dad finally turned to me and said, "You really want me to give your mother money for Christmas presents?"

"You have to," I insisted.

"The only thing I have to do is die and pay taxes," Dad replied and grinned a little. "Okay, if you want me to give your mother some money, you have to let me shoot a cigarette out of your hand." Dad looked at me and tried to hold back his smile, which told me he was bluffing. He said, "What do you say? Do you trust your old man?"

I remember how Dad would always tell us stories about growing up an only child on a farm outside of Detroit during the Depression. That's where he learned to shoot. Dad was modest when he was sober, but after a few beers, he always bragged about what a good marksman he was and how he had shot a cigarette out of a girl's hand once to win a bet. I used to believe him, but I started to doubt the story as I got older, mostly because he would tell this other story about being attacked by a bobcat. Dad claimed he grabbed it by the tail, swung it around his head and threw it off a cliff. Then I learned that Bobcats don't have real tails. He laughed at me when I finally figured it out.

"How much money will you give Ma if I do it?" I asked, calling his bluff. I had played poker with Dad plenty of times. He was a good bluffer, but not when he was drunk.

"Fifty dollars," Dad said, "but you have to give me five dollars if you chicken out."

"I don't have five dollars," I said.

"Okay, then forget it," Dad said.

I knew what he was doing, so I called his bluff again. "Okay, I'll borrow it from Cathy," I said, even though I knew she didn't have that much money.

Dad looked at me and grinned. I started to worry he might not be bluffing. Then he stood up and went into his bedroom. I knew he was going to get a bullet for his rifle. He always warned me that you never store the bullets with a gun if there are kids in the house. But I knew that Dad hid his .22 caliber bullets in his underwear drawer because Billy and Bobby had found them one day when they were playing detectives.

"Grab one of my Lucky Strikes and hold it between your fingers with your arm straight out over there," Dad said as he picked up the rifle and pointed to the kitchen wall behind me.

I remember feeling a little queasy when he started to load the bullet into the rifle. I still didn't believe he'd do it and said, "What if you hit my fingers?"

"Then you won't be able to pick your nose with them anymore."

"Funny," I said, starting to get more scared.

"Trust me, Kevin … but if you wanna chicken out, give me the five dollars now," Dad said, trying to goad me.

I took the bait. I didn't like to lose, and I'd fallen for Dad's bluffs too many times before. I grabbed one of his Lucky Strikes and walked over to the kitchen wall. I stuck my arm out, holding the cigarette up between my index finger and thumb. I breathed out to keep it steady. Dad wasn't going to shoot, but I didn't know how he was going to weasel out of it.

Dad walked down the hallway from the kitchen with the rifle pointed down for safety, like he had taught me to do. I couldn't see him from where I stood because I didn't want to risk the bullet hitting me in the chest or face, just in case Dad was in a crazy enough mood to really try to shoot the cigarette out of my hand.

Then I heard Janie scream, "Ma, get out of the bathroom! Dad's got a gun. He's going to shoot Kevin!"

Everyone came rushing over to the hallway. I moved my head to peek a look at Dad. He was down on one knee about twenty feet away, the .22 against his shoulder, pointed towards my outstretched arm, squinting to line up the Lucky Strike cigarette in the rifle sights. I pulled my head back instantly. I was scared, but I wasn't going to quit the bet.

"Everyone get back!" Dad yelled. "Okay, Kevin, don't move your hand."

I still didn't believe he'd do it. Then I heard the bathroom door open and Ma started to say something. I breathed out, knowing Dad would stop now …

A quick, loud noise like a fire cracker going off sounded suddenly. I flinched but kept my hand still. I felt something tug lightly on it for a split second and then heard a pop in the kitchen wall. Ma screamed, followed by Janie. Sean started to cry.

I whipped my head to look at my hand. The top half of the Lucky Strike cigarette was gone, and there was a small hole in the kitchen wall with plaster dust smoking from it. My fingers were still there.

"Woo-hah!" I yelled and ran down the hallway to show everyone the cigarette. "Great shot, Dad, but now you have to give Ma fifty bucks for presents! Yahoo! Merry Christmas!"

Dad was standing and smirking. He took the shot-off cigarette out of my hand and walked to the kitchen, the .22 pointed down even though it wasn't loaded anymore. He turned his head to look at me and said, "See, I told you to trust me."

"Jesus Christ, Bob!" Ma yelled as she followed us into the kitchen. "Are you crazy? Kevin, are you alright?"

"Yeah, but Dad isn't. He has to give you fifty dollars now to go Christmas shopping."

As soon as the other kids realized I was okay, they went back to what they were doing, which amounted to hiding from the crisis around Christmas that Ma and Dad had created. Janie hovered over Ma while Lynn lingered in the hallway near the kitchen listening to what was being said. Cathy went to her room, I think to cry, and Billy and Bobby went back to singing songs with Debbie and Sean by the Christmas tree. We all had our own ways of protecting ourselves.

I was still wound up as I stood in the kitchen waiting. Dad sat down and laid the .22 on the table. He lit the half shot-off Lucky Strike and began to smoke it.

"I don't have fifty dollars to give your mother," he said without looking at me.

My heart dropped to my stomach. "What? You promised!" I cried.

"I only have fifty on me. I can give your mother forty."

"But you promised fifty," I said, tears starting to form in my eyes.

"Cut it out, Kevin," Dad snapped. "I'll owe your mother ten bucks. She knows I'm good for it." He laughed for a second and then took a drag of his cigarette.

Before I could complain again, Ma snapped at Dad, "Just give me the money so I can send Cathy to the store."

Dad took his money out of his pocket, wet his thumb and counted out four ten dollar bills. I saw that he had two more. Ma told me to get Cathy so she could go to the store before it closed.

When I came back with Cathy, I asked, "Can I go with her? I won the money."

By now, Ma was smoking a cigarette and sipping some beer again, getting ready to call and talk to Nana, her mother and our Grandmother. Ma said, "Okay, but put on a warm coat." I only had one coat. Then Ma gave Cathy twenty of the forty dollars and told her, "Go to Woolworth's. I need some wrapping paper and tape, and I still need a couple of things for Billy, Bobby, Debbie and Sean. Pick something out for them. You better hurry up. They close in half an hour."

I couldn't believe it. I had risked getting my fingers shot off by Dad for twenty dollars. Even in 1968, that didn't buy much for four kids. And I knew that Ma hadn't bought many presents yet. I had already found out where she hid them and looked to see if the new hockey stick I wanted was there. It wasn't.

We had all gotten into the Boston Bruins and hockey recently. We played street hockey rather than ice hockey because we couldn't afford skates or ice time. I was hoping that Ma would tell Cathy to pick up the new hockey stick I wanted for Christmas, but twenty dollars wouldn't have been enough to buy me a new stick and also buy anyone else anything. I had fallen into the Cunningham Christmas trap again—I had let myself want something.

Cathy and I ran the mile uptown and made it to Woolworth's fifteen minutes before closing. It was easy to pick something out for Sean since he was so little. Cathy got Debbie something to do with *Barbie*, and I was left with ten dollars to buy presents for Billy and Bobby. They had also asked for new hockey sticks for Christmas because Bob's had busted during a game and I had broken Billy's while using it in place of my cracked one. He thought I broke it on purpose, but I didn't.

I knew Ma hadn't gotten them hockey sticks either, so that was the first idea I had when I got to the store. Woolworth's was pretty picked over at seven o'clock Christmas Eve. I didn't expect to find any hockey sticks left, so I was shocked when there were two sticks still there in the small sporting goods section. They were a little big for Billy and Bobby, but they had Bobby Orr's signature on them. The problem was they cost eight bucks a piece. I only had ten.

I thought about buying a stick for Billy since I had broken his, but that would have left only two dollars to buy Bobby something. I decided to buy one stick and one puck for the two of them to share.

But when I told Cathy my plan, she said, "That's not fair. They always have to share presents."

I said, "I don't have enough money to buy them each a stick. And they're used to it."

Then Cathy took a five dollar bill and five ones out of her pocket and handed them to me.

I said, "Where'd you get all that?"

She said, "From babysitting. Take it. Merry Christmas."

Billy, Bobby, Debbie and Sean did okay for presents that Christmas morning compared to previous ones. The hockey sticks were a big hit. Cathy and Lynn got mostly cheap clothes, but I don't think they expected much more. Janie was usually happy with whatever she received. I got a few things I wanted, but I was pretty disappointed at not getting a hockey stick. Billy and Bobby actually offered to share their sticks so I could play with them.

I remember Ma was sitting on the couch drinking a cup of tea and watching everyone open the last of their presents. Dad was in his chair watching us too, smoking a cigarette and drinking a cup of coffee. Neither of them had opened the small presents from us yet.

"Kevin, I dropped my lighter behind the couch last night," Dad said to me as I sat on the floor by the tree with my legs crossed, looking at a book I'd gotten. "Check behind there and see if you can find it."

I wasn't in a mood to do anything for anyone, so I didn't respond. I just crawled over to the couch and reached behind it. I felt a long wooden stick and pulled it out. It was a new hockey stick with Derek Sanderson's signature on it. He was my favorite Boston Bruins hockey player.

Dad grinned and said, "I was outside last night and saw a red light moving really fast in the sky. So, I grabbed the 22 and shot at it. I missed but that fell out and landed at my feet."

"Ma, Dad shot at Rudolph," Janie exclaimed.

"He's just kidding, Janie," I said to calm her down.

She said, "Oh, I knew that."

I looked at Dad and smiled. He smirked at me with that self-conscious, warm look he had whenever he felt good about something he'd done. Then he took a long drag of his cigarette.

I guess that's a special memory. Maybe even a good one.

The Fifth Child

BETTING ON CHRISTMAS

When Billy sent me an email about his and Bobby's idea to compile a collection of Cunningham Christmas stories by each of my brothers and sisters into a book to pass along to our children, I replied, "I'm not sure I want to go down that rat hole."

But as I drove along Route 128 with my husband, Phil, I started to feel guilty about my harsh response. It was probably because it was December 23, and Phil and I had just finished visiting my mother and older sister Janie. It was an annual tradition that began when Phil and I first started dating, five years after my divorce. We'd head up to Beverly a couple of days before Christmas to drop off their presents and then take them out to The Danversport Yacht Club for lunch. That and my ten dollar contributions to *Globe Santa* in the name of each of my brothers and sisters were my regular Cunningham family good deeds every Christmas.

It was getting dark as we merged onto I-95 towards Boston. I hated driving at night, but dusk was the worst.

Phil must have sensed my stress and asked me, "Do you want me to drive?"

I said, pretty snippy, "I'm fine."

He replied, "Okay, Ms. Grinch, but I think the steering wheel has stopped breathing from your death grip."

I glanced down for a second. My knuckles were white. I sighed and said, "I'm Sorry."

Phil said tenderly, "It's okay, Lynn. What's wrong?"

I replied, "This stupid Christmas story that Billy and Bobby asked me to write."

"I thought you weren't going to do it," he said.

"I don't know," I replied. "It got me thinking about a lot of things."

"And now you can't stop?" Phil said.

"It just brought back so many bad memories," I said.

Phil said, "So, just stop thinking about them. Think about me."

I looked at him, and he smiled. I smiled back. Then I turned to focus on the road. I said, "It wasn't like it was all bad. I have some good memories too."

Phil said, "Well, it sounds like maybe you want to try to write something. You know, you don't have to share it with anyone if you don't want, except me, of course."

I think he smiled at me again, but I was too busy squinting, trying to see past the oncoming headlights glaring against the cold, fading sky. Did I say I hated driving at dusk?

Phil added, "Maybe you'll feel better after writing something. It can't hurt to try. Right?"

I glanced at him, smiled wryly and said, "You want to bet?"

As I turned my attention back to the road, my words seemed to echo in my head. Dad used to say that all the time. My mind wandered back to Christmas, 1973. It was this exact same day, December 23. I don't know why I suddenly remembered it so clearly, but I did. I was in the middle of watching Gilligan's Island when the phone rang. I heard Ma answer it and talk for a minute. Then she called me to the kitchen and handed me the phone.

She said in an irritated voice, "It's your father."

I rolled my eyes and sighed. It could mean only one thing. Dad needed me to pick him up from work. He had lost his license when he was arrested for drunk driving after crashing into a telephone pole. That might not seem so bad except that he was a truck driver.

Fortunately, the trucking outfit he worked for let him switch jobs. He now worked the dock, loading and unloading the same trucks he used to drive. Unfortunately, he had to work nights, and his company was located over an hour away from Amesbury, Massachusetts, where we lived in a three bedroom apartment at the time. There was no public transportation to his work, and Ma didn't drive.

When Dad first lost his license, we thought he would lose his job for sure. That would have been another Cunningham family disaster, but Dad showed again what he was capable of when his back was to the wall. He decided to try to hitchhike back and forth to work, which was over forty miles each way. It seemed like a crazy idea to all of us when he started. The first couple of days, it took him almost four hours each way. I remember hearing him several times in those first few weeks throwing up in the bathroom from nervousness before he left to try to hitchhike to work. After a couple of weeks, though, he became a fixture on I-495. The regular commuters would stop every night to give him a ride as far as they could. Before long, he was getting back and forth to work in an hour and a half, just a little longer than when he drove himself.

Every weekend when Dad would get drunk with Ma, he'd talk about the different people who had given him lifts that week. There were teachers, accountants, construction workers, truck drivers, white-collar professionals, and even police officers on their way home at the end of a graveyard shift. There was one state trooper who would pick him up regularly and give him a beer from a cooler he kept in the trunk of his police car. They would polish off a couple of cold ones during the ride, talking about sports, local politics, and country and western music. The irony of the situation wasn't lost on Dad, but he always appreciated the help. He was never very judgmental. To him, everyone was just doing what they had to in order to get by.

I took the phone from Ma and said, "Yes?"

"Lynn, I need you to come get me," Dad said loudly.

I could tell he was drunk. I said, "Why don't you get a lift from whoever you're drinking with?"

"Jesus Christ, Lynn," he replied, "just come and pick me up, will ya? If you don't come soon, I won't have any money to give your mother for Christmas shopping."

"Dad, what are you talking about?" I said. "Where are you?"

Dad answered, "I'm at Sal's house having a few beers and playing some cards. It'll only take you a half hour. Your mother's waiting for some money from me. Hurry up."

Sal was one of Dad's friends from work. He lived about twenty miles away in Manchester, New Hampshire. I had picked Dad up at Sal's house twice before. Both times, Dad had lost all the money he had on him playing cards. This was not good.

"Dad, how much have you lost?" I asked, dreading his answer.

"Jesus, Lynn, you sound like your mother," Dad replied.

"I'm not coming to pick you up unless you tell me," I said.

"Twenty bucks," Dad said. "You satisfied? Now, come get me or you'll be to blame if I lose the rest of my paycheck."

Dad only took home about two hundred dollars a week at the time. Twenty dollars was a big bite, especially since Ma still hadn't done any real Christmas shopping for the kids. We didn't even have a Christmas tree yet. Although Dad was pretty good at cards, he always drank when he gambled and eventually made stupid bets and lost. I could see another Cunningham crisis barreling down the road.

I said, "Fine. I'll be there as soon as I can. Don't lose any more money."

Dad slurred, "Don't worry, Lynn. Your old man's got them right where I want them." He laughed, then said seriously, "Be careful driving. It's slippery out. One of the guys here nearly jackknifed on some black ice. Take it easy."

That was typical Dad. He wouldn't give a second thought to doing something stupid himself that might wreck our entire Christmas, but then he'd show this fatherly concern for our safety when he had no control over it. It was like it was alright if he put us in harm's way but not if the rest of the world did. Ma was the same way, just more obsessive about the worrying. They both thrived on crises, most of the time ones that they created. Growing up, it seemed like Christmas was just an excuse for another Cunningham crisis.

As I said, I really hated driving at night. Whenever I had to, I would ask Billy or Bobby to keep me company, but they weren't around. I remember it was cold that night, and the heater wasn't working on Dad's beat-up Ford Falcon. I had just gotten my license and was driving it all the time because Kevin, my older brother, hadn't gotten his license yet and Dad, of course, wasn't supposed to drive. Sometimes, he snuck in a drive in order to get his beer and cigarettes when no one was around to get them for him. He always seemed to be lucky about getting away with idiotic things like that but never the important stuff that affected us.

It was dark, with spitting snow. I was very nervous driving, which made me even more angry at Dad. The more I thought about him, the angrier I got. After the whole court hearing thing last year, it was hard for me to decide if he was a good person who was just really messed up or a bad person who was lucky and likable.

It had been a year and a half since the last time Dad whipped me with a belt. We had all grown up getting the belt when Dad was in a bad mood and Ma was bugging him to punish us for something, which was usually nothing in the scheme of things given what we were exposed to. Ma often instigated the belt whippings of me by telling Dad I had snuck out again at night to go do, in her words, "God knows what." When the parents of one of my friends called the local family services office about Dad, he had to go to court and answer some questions. Nothing ended up happening, but after the court appearance, he never used a belt or hit me again. He had an excuse now not to listen to Ma's complaints. I grew up after that too.

I guess I knew Dad was a good person, but he had a mean streak, probably from the way he grew up. He was more or less abandoned by his real mother when he was born and raised an only child by a Great Aunt and Uncle on a farm outside Detroit during the Depression. He dropped out of school in the eighth grade and got into a lot of trouble, but then he joined the Navy and served in the Korean War. He straightened out for the most part after that. Dad was actually pretty smart. That's probably why he managed to get through so much self-inflicted trouble without getting himself killed.

I remember the previous Christmas had felt strange because of all the commotion around me. But things had gotten better between Dad and me since then. I don't remember him ever saying he was sorry, but he probably didn't think he had done anything that bad. It was the way he had grown up and the only way he knew how to discipline, but it was wrong.

The only thing I was sure of about Dad was that he was a survivor. No matter what life threw at him or he threw at himself, he always managed to figure out a way to get through it. Dad always said to never bet against him because he had a leprechaun sitting on his shoulder looking out for him. If he did, it was a selfish leprechaun, because I never ever felt lucky growing up, especially around Christmas.

That night, however, something changed.

As I turned to take the highway exit towards Sal's house, I hit some black ice and my car started to spin out of control. I remember praying not to die and then hearing Dad's voice saying again what he always told me to do if I started skidding on ice. I turned the steering wheel sharply in the direction that the back of my car was spinning. I started to get control when I slammed into something and stopped abruptly.

No one wore seatbelts back then. I was still okay, but I was pretty shaken up. After calming down, I got out and walked around to the passenger side. I looked and saw that I had run into a pile of old truck tires along the side of the road. They had stopped me from skidding down a steep incline.

I managed to regain my composure by the time I walked into Sal's house. I immediately spotted Dad at the kitchen table in the middle of a card game with five other men. I recognized four of them. They were truck drivers who worked with Dad. He was sitting with his arms crossed and a cigarette dangling from his hand. He looked tired and drunk. A woman I think was Sal's wife and three other men I didn't know were standing around watching the action. The atmosphere was tense. I could tell something big was happening.

I got closer to the table and saw a large pile of money sitting in the center. There was a fifty-dollar bill on top of four or five twenties, with a few tens and fives underneath, all on top of a mound of one-dollar bills. Dave, one of Dad's truck driver friends, was dealing, putting down two cards face up and then waiting for one of the other players to make a bet. They were playing acey-deucey.

"Hi Dad, I'm here," I said and touched him on the shoulder to get his attention.

"Oh, you made it," he said and looked up at me. His brilliant blue eyes were bloodshot and drooping. He asked, "How was the driving?"

"Bad," I answered. "I nearly skidded off the highway."

Dave looked up from dealing and said, "Was that right off the exit coming here? Sal said a truck skidded off the road there earlier today and lost a bunch of old tires."

"Yeah, I think I ran into them," I replied. "They stopped me from going off the road."

Dave said, "You were lucky you weren't hurt. That driver's supposedly in the hospital. You must have an angel looking out for you."

Dad asked, "My car okay?"

I sighed and said, "Yeah. I am too. Are you ready to go?"

"I gotta introduce you first," he slurred. He turned and announced to the table, "Hey, this is my daughter, Lynn. She's not just good looking. She can type a hundred and twenty words a minute too."

"The company should fire Doris and hire your daughter, Bob," Sal declared from across the table, prompting a collective laugh from everyone for a second before they all turned their attention back to the game.

I looked down at the table in front of Dad and saw six dollars lying there. I asked him in a low, panicked voice, "Dad, that's not all you have left, is it?"

"No," he replied and took a puff of his cigarette. "Have a little faith, will ya."

I breathed a sigh of relief.

Then Dad said, "See all that money in the middle? That's mine too, as soon as I build up enough to bet the pot. Your old man's feeling lucky."

My mouth opened to say something but nothing came out. Dad had lost his entire paycheck, except for six dollars. There would be no Christmas presents, no tree, no food, and no rent. Blood rushed to my face, and I felt my heart pounding. Dad had bet our Christmas on a game of acey-deucey and lost.

"Ooohhh!"

A collective groan came from the other players and the people watching. I looked down at the table and saw a jack of spades and a three of diamonds face up with a two of clubs in between them. The guy to Dad's right was swearing as he took the ten dollar bill he had bet and tossed it onto the growing pot.

"You're up, Bob," Dave said and put down a king of hearts and a three of spades, leaving a space in between for the next card that Dad would have to either bet on before it was shown or pass to the next player. Dave added, "That's a pretty good bet, Bob."

I knew Dad would probably win if he bet, but he could only win six dollars since that's all he had left to bet. It would take him all night to win back what he had lost, and that was assuming he won every hand from there. Believing he could do that was probably how he got so far down to begin with. Dad's luck was too little too late to save our Christmas.

Dad rubbed his hand over the stubble on his chin while he contemplated what to do. He looked around the table with a smirk on his face and asked loudly, "Anybody wanna spot me for a cut of the pot?"

I couldn't believe what I was hearing! Dad was going to borrow over two hundred dollars to bet the pot on one card. If he lost, his next paycheck would be gone too. If he drew a three or a king, matching either of the two cards showing, he would have to pay double the pot!

I leaned over his shoulder, looked him in the eyes and said, "What are you doing, Dad? You have to stop. You've already ruined Christmas. You can't afford to lose any more money."

"Hush, Lynn," he said. "Your old man's ship just came in. I just need someone to stake me."

Dad looked around and asked a couple of the drivers who worked with him, but they all declined. Nobody wanted to have to try to collect the money from Dad if he lost.

"I'll stake ya, Bob," a voice shouted from the back of the kitchen. It was Frank, Dad's best friend who was a driver for another trucking company. Murmurs of surprise came from the other players around the table. My heart sank.

Frank stepped up to the table, clearly drunk. He was a big man, especially compared to Dad, who was all of five foot five and a half inches. Frank threw down two fifties and six twenties next to Dad, then bellowed, "I'm up a lot tonight and most of it's your money." He laughed and added, "I don't mind doubling down for you. Happy Hanukkah, Bob."

Dad smirked and straightened up, then clapped his hands and rubbed them together. He said, "Deal the card so I can win and get going."

A few of the other drivers laughed at Dad's bravado, but most of them just watched anxiously, knowing how bad it would be if Dad lost. I remember closing my eyes, holding my breath and praying, just like I had a half hour ago spinning out of control on the highway.

Then loud cheers and shouts erupted in the room. I opened my eyes and looked down at the table. A four of diamonds was sitting between the king of hearts and three of spades. I breathed out. Dad had won!

I looked at Dad. He was grinning, a cigarette hanging from his mouth now. He turned and looked up at me. I leaned down so I could hear what he was going to say.

He took the cigarette out of his mouth and said, "See, you brought me good luck."

I was still shaking from adrenaline as I pulled onto the highway headed home with Dad in the passenger seat. I glanced at him. He was staring blankly at the oncoming highway, almost as if he was driving a truck, with a slight, contented smile on his lips.

I said to him, "I'm not going to tell Ma about this."

Dad looked at me and said, "Go ahead and tell her. I won, didn't I?"

I shot him an exasperated look and said, "You're unbelievable. You bet our Christmas on a card game. What if you had lost, Dad?"

He smirked and said, "Haven't I always told you never bet against your old man?"

I just shook my head and didn't respond. I noticed him with my peripheral vision watching me.

He shrugged his shoulders and said, "Sorry. Wake me when we get home." He leaned against the passenger door and curled up, almost like a little boy. After a few minutes, he muttered, "Thanks Lynn."

That Christmas turned out okay after all, but it was hard for me to really enjoy it because I knew we had missed a disaster by just one card. As I write this now, I have to believe there really was something else at work that night. Maybe my prayers did have something to do with it. Or maybe God was there all along and just decided it was time to give us Cunningham kids a break. I like to think it was both. It's funny, I had forgotten how I felt back then until now.

Phil and I were almost home when I realized I hadn't said anything in a while. I glanced over at him and smiled.

He said, "Everything okay? You kind of zoned out there."

I replied, "Yeah. I was just thinking about the Christmas story I'm going to write."

He said, "Is it a good one or another one of those crazy Cunningham stories?"

I laughed and said, "Both, of course."

The Sixth Child

A WHISPER OF CHRISTMAS

I never lived a Cunningham Christmas, but I experienced and loved them all, through my sisters and brothers. But that was a long time ago.

Now, as I watch, I worry. I worry that my brothers and sisters have forgotten, that their memories of growing up together have faded and darkened, and with this, the hope and resilience that has kept me alive all these years. I worry that what was good in my family is dying.

I could not let that happen. So I whispered, as we sometimes do, and I prayed, as we often do, that my sisters and brothers would hear me. I whispered and asked each of them to remember a Christmas growing up and to record that memory in a story. I whispered and asked them each to write a verse of *The Twelve Children of Christmas*, to create a collection of our family Christmas memories, so that the hope of their childhoods would live on, for their children and their families. I asked them each to remember, and each of them heard me.

You may wonder why Christmas was so important, especially to children who were barely given religion or gifts. The answer is that Christmas to us was pure hope—the hope of children. It was all we had and all we could count on. No big presents or magical spectacle or spiritual redemption. Hope bound us as a family, and I knew that if each of my brothers and sisters tried to remember a Christmas growing up, that hope would be rekindled. My family would live again, through Christmas memories, and so would I.

There were twelve of us, *The Twelve Children of Christmas*, all different verses but the same refrain—hope. We were children once, together, a long time ago, but we will be a family forever, as long as we remember.

Merry Christmas everyone!!!!!!!!!!!!

* * *

Stacy Ellen Cunningham was born March 8, 1958, in Boston, Massachusetts. She died in Boston on July 8, 1958, of *crib death*, now known as *sudden infant death syndrome*, or SIDS. Sadly for us, her eleven brothers and sisters, Stacy never experienced a Cunningham Christmas.

The Seventh Child

IT'S ONLY
A CARDBOARD CHRISTMAS

"You're going to have to break up that roadblock sometime," Debbie warned Danny as she handed him the dice. "When you do, I'm going to get my revenge!"

"Come on, why don't you move your men?" Sean added. "Roadblocks make the game boring!"

Danny looked up at me and asked, "Bobby, should I move them?"

I shook my head and told him, "Not yet. You want to get your other two men around the board as far as you can before you break it up. Don't listen to them. If they had the chance, they would be blockading you. It's just part of the strategy."

Parcheesi is a fun game … for most families. For our family, it was a competitive sport. From the first roll of the dice, it was a no-holds-barred, take-no-prisoners battle. We might start out with the idea of having a fun, light-hearted game, but eventually, the competitive Cunningham spirit would kick in, and it would become a scratching and clawing race to the finish.

It was the first week in December and the six younger members of the family were seated at the kitchen table playing Parcheesi after a satisfying spaghetti dinner. Danny, who was almost five, was my partner and was sitting next to me on a long bench on one side of the table. On the other side were Billy, Erika, and Debbie. Erika, who was only eighteen months old, was sitting on Billy's lap as his partner. She was too young to fully understand the object of the game but enjoyed rolling the dice and trying to get doubles so she could roll again. Sean, the last of the combatants, was at the head of the table, in between the two groups.

I was teaching Danny how to play the game, and much to the frustration of Sean and Debbie, he had mastered the art of blockades. Their pieces were backed up behind two of his men, preventing them from moving. Sean was eight and thought he was a Parcheesi pro. For the life of him, he couldn't understand how he was stuck behind a five-year-old's roadblock. At twelve years old, Debbie had learned the virtue of patience in Parcheesi but was still getting frustrated after rolling doubles twice without being able to move.

Billy and I were passing secret glances to coordinate a strategy that would protect both Danny and Erika. At fourteen, we were the oldest of this group of siblings and felt it our responsibility to make sure the younger kids had a fighting chance to win. Given how competitive these Parcheesi games could get, Danny and Erika needed some kind of advantage.

"*Santa Claus is Coming to Town* is coming on!" Janie yelled from the living room.

There was a mad scramble as Debbie, Sean, Danny, and Erika jumped up from their seats and dashed into the living room, diving for their favorite spots in front of the TV. The Parcheesi game was important, but Christmas specials like *Santa Claus is Coming to Town* only came on television once a year. It was 1973 and there were no VCRs, DVRs, or DVDs. If you didn't catch them when they came on, you had to wait another year to watch them.

During the mass exodus, someone had smacked into the edge of the Parcheesi board, sending the game flying into the air. The board landed on the bench while most of the playing pieces bounced across the table and onto the kitchen floor like balls on a roulette wheel.

"Hey! You guys just knocked over the entire game. Come back and help clean up the mess," I yelled to the four of them, but they had already claimed their territory on the floor or the couch. And they were not going to risk losing a prime viewing spot. So Billy and I quickly collected the scattered pieces, packed up the game, and then sprinted out to join them right as the show was starting.

We had just finished watching the part where Santa, to avoid detection by the evil Burgermeister, came up with the idea of using chimneys to deliver his presents. During the commercial break, Danny asked, "How can Santa come if we don't have a fireplace?"

Our family lived in a shabby apartment on the first floor of an old, three-story Victorian house. There were three bedrooms, a kitchen with a pantry, one living room and one bathroom ... but no fireplace.

"Don't worry, Danny," I told him. "Not having a fireplace won't stop Santa from coming. It's too important to him to visit you on Christmas and deliver your presents. When there's no chimney to come down, he just comes in through the door or window. Even if they're locked, Santa has magical abilities that allow him to open them."

"Well, then why does every story show him coming down the chimney?" Sean asked. He was older than Danny and wanted a more realistic reason to believe in this stuff. A standard explanation wouldn't do. I had to pull out my best Christmas logic.

"Well, Sean, in the olden days when Santa first started delivering presents, the fireplace was like the center of your house. That's where you would cook, where you would get warm, and where everyone would gather as a family. Everything happened around the fireplace. When families woke up Christmas morning and found the presents Santa had left, they tried to figure out how he had entered their house. With the doors and windows locked, the first place they thought of, naturally, was the chimney. Maybe he used the chimney, maybe he didn't. Maybe he used his magic to enter some other way, but the mystery of how he does it is part of what makes Christmas so much fun."

Sean's brow was wrinkled with thought as he considered the plausibility of my story. Before he could decide if he believed me, the commercials ended and *Santa Claus is Coming to Town* was back on.

When the program ended, the conversation shifted from questioning how Santa did what he did to a wistful discussion of how great it would be if we had our own fireplace. Sean and Danny went back and forth with their plans for how they would build one. Even Debbie, who had been silent during most of the Santa Claus discussion, got excited by this topic, describing in detail how she would decorate the mantel and pile the wood to make a perfect fire. Erika kept clapping her hands together saying, "Firepace! Firepace!" like she was cheering on a football team.

Then Janie suggested that with Dad's help, maybe we could build a real fireplace. Sean and Danny stopped talking and looked at each other with mouths agape and eyes wide open at this exciting prospect. Erika squealed her approval and continued her fireplace cheer. Then all of them started talking at the same time, making plans for where the fireplace would be and what it would look like. Before their enthusiasm ran away with them, I had to explain how unrealistic the idea was.

"Hold on guys! Before you get too excited, there's really no way we can do this. It costs a lot of money—thousands of dollars—and takes a long time, like months, to build a real fireplace with a chimney. We'd have to tear down a wall too. And I'm not sure Dad really knows how to build one …"

I could see their faces drop as they listened to my explanation. A huge wave of guilt swept over me as I realized I had just squashed one of the few wishes they dared to have for Christmas. Sure, I was just trying to manage their expectations so they wouldn't be too disappointed when it didn't happen. But for a family like ours, sometimes wishes were all we had for Christmas. Not having wishes was like not having hope. I had to figure out some way to make it better.

"But you know …" I started saying, figuring out a plan in my mind as I talked, "we can still have a fireplace even if it isn't a real one. We can build a fake one—not a fake one like a toy one—I mean something that looks real even if it isn't made of bricks. We can make it out of wood or cardboard with a mantel for stockings and a chimney and everything. We can even make a fake fire that looks real."

"But can Santa come down a fake chimney?" Danny asked.

"Sure he can!" Billy chimed in. "Remember what we were talking about before? Santa has magical abilities. He can come down a chimney even when there's a fire in the fireplace, and he can even visit homes that don't have a fireplace or chimney. I'm sure if he needs to, he can figure out how to come down a pretend chimney."

"That's right," I added. "Santa will certainly figure out some way to come down our chimney. It will be fun to build it, and it will make everything more Christmasy!"

"Yah, that would be wicked cool!" Sean said, warming up to the idea. "Maybe we can even figure out a way to have a real fire in the fireplace."

"Well, even if we can't do a real fire, we can still make it look like a real fire just like they do in the movies," I said, trying to avoid a future visit by the fire department.

"We can have cocoa and pretend we're roasting marshmallows over the fire," Debbie said.

"And we can sing Christmas songs in front of the fireplace too!" Janie added.

Everyone was back to being excited about Christmas. Sean and Danny grabbed some paper and pencils and went out to the kitchen table to start drafting their plans for what the fireplace should look like. Erika joined them, doing her best to imitate their drawing actions, and Janie went to look through some magazines to find pictures of fireplaces that we could use for our design.

"Good luck with the fireplace," Debbie said. "If you need any help, I'll probably be busy." She smiled as she headed back to the couch to continue watching TV.

I turned to Billy and said, "Well, we have our work cut out for us, but if we can build this, the kids are going to love it."

The next day, after school, we put our plan into action. We didn't have any wood, so the fireplace would have to be made out of cardboard. I went to the A&P grocery store and managed to get a few sturdy boxes, making sure they didn't have a lot of printing on them. Our idea was to color the cardboard to look like bricks, so the boxes had to be as plain as possible.

We lucked out by getting a big box from a neighbor who had just purchased a new television. Together with the boxes from the A&P, we had just enough cardboard to build the main fireplace itself. There wasn't enough for a chimney, but there was still plenty of time before Christmas to find some more boxes.

Over the next couple of weeks we worked on the fireplace as often as we could, in between school, homework, and the frequent neighborhood street-hockey games. Like most projects when you're a kid, it turned out to be a lot more work than we expected. Creating the look of real brick was the biggest challenge. Crayons alone did not produce the desired effect, so we had to color the cardboard again using a mixture of red and brown water-color paints.

It took over two weeks to finish building the fireplace. The final product looked pretty good, but it was now Christmas Eve day, and we didn't have a chimney or a fire yet. It was going to be a tight race to see if we could finish before Santa arrived.

While Billy went to the A&P to see if he could scrounge up some more boxes, I started the process of making a fake fire with some help from Sean, Danny, and Erika. Sean taped together two toilet paper rolls end-to-end and then covered each open end with paper. Then Danny painted it brown and scrunched it up to make it look like a fireplace log. Erika performed the final check to make sure it looked like real wood.

We made five of them and then tied them together with brown sewing thread. Next, Sean and Danny made the flames by drawing and coloring them on white paper. I cut them out and taped them to the logs, overlapping them to create a 3-D effect. My plan was to put a flashlight behind the flames to make them glow like a real fire.

The fireplace and fire were ready, but we were still missing a chimney. Billy had struck out finding more boxes at the A&P, so we decided to check at the local liquor store—the one my parents visited all too often. We were in luck! They had extra boxes. But they had beer designs on them, which we couldn't hide with crayons or paint. Fortunately, we had some red construction paper we used to cover them. I'm not sure what Santa would have thought about a chimney with a *Pabst Blue Ribbon Beer* label on the front.

Billy and I were still working on the chimney when it was time for the younger kids to go to bed. I promised them everything would be done in time for Santa's arrival. Then we sang them some Christmas songs and tucked them in for a long winter's nap.

Around eleven o'clock, we finally finished the fireplace and placed it up against the wall on the opposite side of the living room from the Christmas tree. Then we attached the chimney on top using strips of masking tape placed discretely so they couldn't be seen. For the final touch, we put the fake fire in the hearth and placed the flashlight behind it. All that was left was to hang the stockings.

Using the few treats that we had—candy canes, walnuts, apples, and some miscellaneous Christmas candy—we filled nine old socks and laid them out in a row on the coffee table. I took the first one and attached it to the mantel using a thumbtack. Billy grabbed the second one and did the same. Suddenly, the fireplace lurched forward from the weight of the stockings and smashed onto the floor, breaking apart from the chimney!

Fortunately, nothing was seriously damaged. We took off the stockings and reassembled the fireplace and chimney. It wasn't quite as pristine as before, but it still looked okay.

Billy and I stood staring at the fireplace, trying to figure out how to prevent the weight of the stockings from pulling it down. The obvious solution was to nail it to the wall, but we knew that the landlord didn't want a bunch of holes in the wall. So we decided instead to use Scotch tape. Fifteen minutes and half a role later, the fireplace was secured to the wall.

We hung up the first four stockings, and everything seemed to be working fine. After attaching the fifth stocking, however, the fireplace and chimney started to pull away from the wall, ripping off the tape and some chunks of plaster. We rushed over and pushed the fireplace and chimney back against the wall. Then we removed both the stockings and tape. Back to the drawing board.

We thought about using thumbtacks since they weren't technically nails. But we ruled them out because they wouldn't be long enough to penetrate the wall through the cardboard. It was past midnight now, and there was only one solution left. The landlord would not be happy, but we had to nail the fireplace to the wall. If it didn't work, we'd have to forego hanging the stockings altogether.

After banging in the nails as quietly as possible, we grabbed two of Kevin's ten-pound barbell weights and leaned them inside the fireplace against the back of the cardboard for extra support. One-by-one, we attached the stockings. When the last one was hung, we stepped back cautiously, ready to pounce forward if the fireplace started to fall again. It stayed still. I tugged on it lightly to test its stability, but it stayed firm. Success! Billy and I each let out a victory yell, and then quickly hushed each other simultaneously.

It took a good minute or two before the adrenaline started to fade and I realized what we had in front of us. With all the worry about it falling over, I hadn't stopped to appreciate how truly amazing the fireplace looked. The fake fire in the hearth, illuminated by the flashlight, shone with a soft glow of red, orange, and yellow flames. With the nine old stockings hanging by the chimney with care, it looked like a scene from a nineteenth-century Christmas. We had set out to create a magical experience for the younger kids and wound up creating some magic for ourselves as well.

We each grabbed one of the oatmeal cookies intended for Santa and sat down in front of the fireplace. We ate the cookies and drank some milk while we listened to Christmas songs on the radio. Nat King Cole was singing about chestnuts roasting on an open fire. At that moment, Christmas was perfect. The worry about being able to buy presents for the kids was behind us, and the disappointment because the presents were too few had not yet happened. The true meaning of Christmas was right in front of us, captivating us with its creativity and hope.

We lingered for a while, enjoying the fireplace and the music, but then it was time to get ready for Christmas morning. I emptied the ashtrays filled with the crushed remnants of a day's worth of chain smoking by Ma and Dad. Billy collected the empty quart bottles of Pabst Blue Ribbon beer, along with the dirty glasses, then brought them to the kitchen and rinsed them out. The bottles would be returned to the liquor store at a later date for their nickel deposits.

I placed an empty glass of milk next to a plate with a few cookie crumbs on it to give the full impression of a visit from Saint Nick. If Santa did make it to our humble apartment, there was a full plate of cookies wrapped up on the kitchen table and a little milk in the refrigerator to feed himself and his crew. I cinched up the belt of my old robe and stuck my hands in the pockets as I turned and gave one last look to the Christmas tree and the fireplace. Then we headed off to bed.

CRASH!

A loud noise jolted me from an exhausted sleep. I sat up, breathing the deep gasps of someone who had just gone from complete rest to instant adrenaline rush. I tried to figure out what had shaken me from my sleep. *The fireplace ... it must have fallen again!*

I leaped out of bed and rushed to the living room, with Billy close behind. We found the fireplace intact—a picture-perfect Christmas scene ... except for the tree. It was lying sideways, half on the TV and half on my mother's old, worn-out armchair. Water from the stand had spilled all over the floor and rug. There were a couple of broken bulbs too, and tinsel was everywhere. But the lights were still shining, so I knew we could fix it.

Then we heard rustling and clawing noises coming from inside the tree! Suddenly, a gray paw reached out from between several branches, followed by a head. It was Spooky, our cat, and apparently our Christmas gremlin too. She was stuck and clawing frantically to get out.

Kevin, Lynn, and Janie all came running out to see what the commotion was, just in time to help free Spooky and right the tree. Lynn went to make sure Sean, Danny, and Erika hadn't woken up, while Kevin, Billy, and I finished adjusting the ornaments and garland. Janie went to check on Ma, which led to Dad yelling at her to go back to bed. She came back out crying. I calmed her down by asking her to help me refill the tree stand with water. Then we all headed back to bed for whatever sleep we could manage before the sun came up.

When Sean, Danny, and Erika jumped on us—Billy and I shared a twin bed—just after six in the morning, I thought someone was pulling a cruel joke. After closing my eyes at 1:30 and being awoken two hours later for tree repair, I had managed only four hours of sleep, not nearly enough for a growing fourteen-year-old. It took every ounce of effort I could muster to reciprocate their enthusiasm. I took a couple of deep breaths, pulled myself out of bed, put on my robe, and stumbled out to the Christmas morning chaos.

To my surprise, Erika, Danny, and Sean were not rummaging through the pile of Christmas presents under the tree. Instead, they were kneeling in front of the fireplace, examining every detail of it with awe. They looked up the chimney, eyeing it to calculate whether it was actually big enough for a rotund Santa to slide down. Then they took turns sprawling in front of the fire to capture the full effect of the glowing Christmas hearth. After that, they each peeked into their stockings to see what treasures awaited them. Finally, they all sat down in front of the fireplace, talking and laughing while they pretended to warm themselves by the flames. It was like a Norman Rockwell scene, or, as the Christmas song goes, "... *a picture print by Currier and Ives.*"

When we finally got around to opening presents, it was a frenzied scene with wrapping paper flying through the air as everyone tore open their gifts as fast as possible. The younger kids got some good presents, relatively speaking, because the older siblings always made an effort to make sure they had something special under the tree on Christmas morning. Billy and I each got a new superblade for our hockey sticks, along with a winter hat and some mittens. The hat and mittens were in a brown paper bag with a Christmas tag on it because Ma had fallen asleep, or passed out, before she could wrap them properly. It wasn't much, but it really didn't matter because I had already gotten what I wanted for Christmas when I saw how much the kids enjoyed their fireplace.

Dad pulled himself out of bed around nine o'clock and came out to join the Christmas morning activities. Erika, Danny, and Sean rushed over to show him our new fireplace. At first, he made some *Scrooge*-like comment that it was only made of cardboard, but then caught himself and said that it looked pretty real and was big enough that even he could come down it. Laughing, the kids went back to exploring their new Christmas presents.

I shook my head at Dad's lack of Christmas spirit, but then I started thinking about what he said. He was right—it was only a cardboard fireplace. But what it meant to us was as real as anything we got that Christmas. It meant fun, it meant hope, and it meant taking care of each other during the many hard times we went through. In truth, the fireplace was a reminder of what was real and what was important for our family.

Erika, Danny, and Sean played with the fireplace for many days and weeks after that. It got beaten up and knocked over and a little more ragged each day. Eventually, they stopped playing with it, and Billy and I decided it was time to take it apart and dispose of it. We considered storing it in the basement until next year, but it was just too "well loved" to survive another Christmas season.

But when Erika, Danny, and Sean got wind of our intentions, they were in an uproar. How could we ever consider taking down this part of Christmas and disposing of it? Sure, it was the beginning of February and they hadn't played with it for almost three weeks, but to them, it was like throwing away Rudolph just because it wasn't Christmas anymore. They wanted to keep it up for as long as possible, like a real fireplace, maybe even until next year. It didn't matter that it was bent and crooked and the chimney was now tilting to one side. They didn't see any of those imperfections. All they saw when they looked at it was the magic of Christmas.

We went along with their wishes for another couple of weeks until it was all but falling down from wear and tear. I explained to them that just like a Christmas tree, the fireplace still had the spirit of Christmas but it needed to be taken down. I promised them we could always build another one next year. We spent one last night playing Parcheesi in front of it while we drank hot cocoa and ate some homemade peanut butter cookies.

Later that night, after Erika, Danny, and Sean were in bed, it was time to take down our Christmas magic. But this was not just an old decoration to be crumpled up and casually thrown away. To us, it was like the U.S. flag. It needed to be disposed of with a respect that matched its importance to us.

Billy and I carefully took it apart and piled up the pieces in a neat stack at the end of the driveway where the town garbage collectors could pick it up. As I stood looking at the remnants of our creation lying there in the cold, February night, I'm sure I saw the spirit of Christmas slowly escaping from the beaten-up, corrugated cardboard. I wished it a final Merry Christmas and headed back inside.

"Daddy, do you still believe in Santa Claus?" my oldest daughter, Katie, asked me. She was almost eleven years old and already questioning whether or not Santa was real.

"Of course I do!" I replied.

"But how can you when most grown-ups don't?" she asked.

"How do you know they don't?" I asked, trying to deflect her real question.

"Because all my friends say their parents don't," she replied. "Come on, Daddy, do you really believe in Santa?"

"Okay, I'll tell you," I said and smiled at her. "Yes, I really do believe in Santa Claus. I always have and always will. I don't know if he's magical and has flying reindeer and elves for helpers. That would be cool, but I don't know for sure. I believe in the idea of Santa and all the good things that he represents. I hope he's all those other things too, but the idea of Santa is what counts. Do you understand what I mean?"

"Mmm, kind of …" Katie replied, scrunching up her nose.

"Let me see if I can explain it a different way," I said. "A long time ago when I was a kid, your Uncle Bill and I built a fireplace for Christmas. It wasn't a real fireplace. It was just a cardboard one …"

I told her the story of our fireplace and what it had meant to me, Billy, and my younger brothers and sisters during that Christmas a long time ago. I explained to her that even though it wasn't a real fireplace, the idea that it represented was as real as the bricks in the fireplace of our current home. That idea was the importance of family, the same idea that Santa represented to me. I told her that it was easy for me to still believe in Santa because I always believed in family.

Katie contemplated my story for a few seconds and then said excitedly, "Can we make a cardboard fireplace like the one you made when you were a kid? That would be so cool!"

Megan, Katie's younger sister who had joined to listen to the story, chimed in, "We could make a big one for ourselves and a little one for our stuffed animals and our American Girl dolls!"

Declan, their four year old younger brother came over and said, "I need one too for my Power Rangers!"

Apparently, my elegant explanation for why I still believed in Santa Claus was not nearly as compelling as the idea of building a cardboard fireplace.

"Why do you want to build a cardboard fireplace when we have a real one?" I asked them.

Katie explained, "It's not the same as building our *own* fireplace."

"And getting to design the way it looks will be so much fun!" Megan added.

"Can we? Can we?" the three of them asked simultaneously.

There was only one answer, of course.

They all ran to the kitchen to tell their mom about their exciting idea to build a fireplace. I laughed at the thought of doing it all over again. I had made that cardboard fireplace over thirty years ago, but I was still learning things from it. And now my kids would too. I guess you cherish something a lot more when you actually make it yourself. Buying your Christmas is never as real as making your Christmas—making it for your family, and yourself.

The Eighth Child

THE TAKING DOWN
OF CHRISTMAS

I don't believe much in God. I never did. So, it's a little interesting, if not strange, that Christmas was so important to me growing up, and still is.

Probably like most kids, the idea of God and Christ was really a grown-up thing that I neither questioned nor worried very much about. The difference between me and most kids, though, was that I never went to church once growing up. Well, there was technically one time. I'll tell you about that in a moment. But Christmas really had nothing to do with religion for me as a kid. It was about hope and family. I guess that's why it's still so important to me.

As I reflect to write this, I have to say that Christmas was always like the first half of a Charles Dickens' story—expectations shattered by the miserable human condition—but with the comforting redemptive ending left out. Truly, my Christmas memories are more like war stories of a band of brothers and sisters, twelve of us, spread over time, surviving and managing to create something out of less than nothing to get by on, because that's what children do.

There is no one Christmas for me growing up so memorable that I would separate it from all the others. Each was a unique, extraordinary creation in its own right. But they were clearly all from the same artists—just permutations, if you will, of the same desperate and damaged visions of life splattered on canvases of time.

The one I've chosen to recount is not exceptional in its darkness or inspiration. I'm sure most, maybe all, of the stories from my brothers and sisters will achieve that better than mine. My story is more about revelation and acceptance, a single Christmas moment when everything was finally simple and clear.

Christmas Eve, 1974—I had just turned fifteen three weeks earlier. It was late, and I was wrapping some last minute presents at the kitchen table, waiting for my older sister Janie to finish getting ready to attend the midnight service at the Baptist Church in downtown Amesbury. Since Janie had some special needs, Ma had asked me and my twin brother Bob if we would accompany her to make sure she got there and back safely.

Ma and Dad were drinking beers and watching television quietly. It was uncharacteristically subdued for the night before Christmas in the Cunningham apartment. But there was good reason. Dad had been arrested for drunk driving two weeks earlier, his second time, which meant he would likely lose his license for five years. He had already lost it once for a year after driving drunk into a telephone pole. He had only gotten it back nine months ago. Dad was a truck driver, you see. His license was his living—the only security our family had.

The first time Dad lost his license, the trucking outfit he worked for had let him take the night shift on the loading dock so he could keep his job. He had somehow managed to hitchhike the forty plus miles to work each night and back for the year his license was suspended. Bob and I used to alternate getting up at four in the morning over the course of that year to have a beer and some food waiting for him when he got home, along with a chess board. We had taken up chess that year and, surprisingly, Dad got into it as well. I would let him win more often than not to make him feel good before he collapsed into bed. What Dad endured that year was an incredible, even admirable, feat. But we all paid a price, not just him.

Thanks to some cheap lawyer, Dad's court hearing for his second drunk driving offense was put off a couple of months. I knew there was little hope of him escaping without having his license suspended for a long time. And I knew Dad wouldn't be able to hitchhike again like he had before. It had taken too much out of him. It meant we would have to move again—the fourth time in ten years—to someplace that had transportation for Dad to get to work, assuming he kept his job.

That was the reason for the dour holiday mood hanging over the Cunningham family. But I was determined not to let it destroy Christmas for my younger brothers and sisters—Erika, Danny, Sean and Debbie. At fifteen, my life had been a blurry progression of taking on greater and greater responsibility every year for them, and increasingly Ma and Dad. The pressure seemed constant, like I was the parent, particularly to Erika and Danny, the youngest ones. I know it was the same for Bob.

After the previous Christmas, which had been another Cunning-ham masterpiece, I had vowed to myself that my younger brothers and sisters would have at least a good Christmas every year. My determina-tion would not ultimately be enough—another hard lesson growing up—but I learned that any effort made a difference, especially that year.

Bob and I knew we needed to earn some money if we wanted to make sure there were enough presents under the tree for the younger ones to have a good Christmas. But the country was in the middle of a bad recession. There were hardly any jobs for adults, never mind two burgeoning fifteen year-olds. Despite this, we managed somehow to find a job that we shared delivering promotional newspapers at a penny a paper.

Amesbury was an old, rural factory town with lots of hills. We could never afford bikes, so we ended up walking miles and miles every week for two months to earn a grand total of about fifty dollars between us. It was a job from hell and made me think about what Dad must have endured in hitchhiking back and forth to work every day for a year.

It still wasn't enough money, but Nana, our grandmother who lived in the projects in South Boston, gave us twenty dollars to help out. With Nana's contribution and the money we had made, there was enough to buy several decent presents for each of our younger brothers and sisters.

My older brother Kevin, who was heading off to the Army soon, had also bought presents for everyone. And even Ma had done some Christmas shopping. It wasn't enough, as usual, but it was something, and more than previous years. I wasn't sure how anyone else would fare

Christmas morning, but I was confident Erika, Danny, Sean and Debbie would do okay.

At bedtime, Bob read *The Night Before Christmas* to the four of them while I snuck outside and jingled some bells to pretend Rudolph was watching. Then I came back in and sang Christmas carols with everyone. Although Debbie was too old for all that stuff and Sean, at nine, thought he was too, they both went along. At two and five-years old, Erika and Danny believed everything and thought it was all magical. Despite the looming, inevitable family crisis, it was looking like it might be a pretty good Christmas. But I wouldn't allow myself to enjoy anything just yet. I had made that mistake too many times before.

After I wrapped the last of the presents we had bought, Bob and I walked Janie to her church for the midnight Christmas service. That was the first church service I had ever attended. The minister said a few religious things to start and then played a slide show of his trip to Bethlehem some years earlier. When he was done, the congregation sang a series of Christmas songs. It was simply beautiful.

I wasn't then and will never be religious, but as I sat there and experienced it for the first time in my life, I understood how people would be drawn to church for services as joyful, spiritual and warm as this one. I've attended numerous services in other churches since. I should have stopped after my first.

It had been a warm night for late December when Janie, Bob and I walked into church, but when we came out, the temperature had dropped well below freezing. I had listened to the forecast on television earlier, hoping for snow, but we were supposed to get clear and unseasonably warm weather for the next few days. Still, the weather-man had already been wrong about the temperature, and this was New England. So, I held onto a sliver of hope that it might snow. I looked up as we started to walk home and blew out, watching my breath freeze against the cold, starlit sky. Not a cloud in sight. Oh well, at least it finally felt like Christmas.

"You guys should have lit a candle in church," Janie said as she walked in between Bob and me down Cedar Street past the old, decaying hat factory, deserted since the Depression. "You get to make a Christmas wish when you do."

"Now you tell me," I said. Although I already knew, I still asked, "What did you wish for?"

Janie answered, "You know what I want—an autographed picture of Lee Majors." He was the star of the television show *The Six Million Dollar Man*, and she was infatuated with him.

"You're dumping Ken Berry for Lee Majors? I can't believe you!" Bob said to her jokingly. Ken Berry was another actor she had been in love with before Lee Majors came along.

"Love 'em and leave 'em Janie," I remarked, laughing.

"No, I still like him … I just like Lee Majors better," Janie replied, a little nervous.

"It's okay, Janie. We're just teasing you," I said.

"I know you are," Janie said and smiled, a little uncertain. Then she asked, "What did you guys wish for from Santa?"

"I wished for him to bring you an autographed picture of Lee Majors," Bob replied and gave Janie a one-armed hug while we turned onto Poplar Street where we lived.

"I wished for a white Christmas … with Lee Majors," I said and gave her a one-armed hug from the other side.

She laughed and said, "I'd like that too." She looked up and added, "But there has to be clouds for it to snow."

I remember the three of us walking towards our first floor apartment in the old, three-story Victorian that sat across the street from a hulking, abandoned brick factory, both of them silhouetted against the dark, clear Christmas night at one o'clock in the morning. The multicolored lights on our tree shone through the window of our front room, along with the glow of the television.

Ma had fallen asleep in her chair but woke up when we came into the room. Dad had already gone to bed. Ma stood up, saying she still had a few gifts to wrap, but Bob and I said we'd finish them. She lay down on the couch and immediately fell asleep. Then Janie went off to bed.

I made some cocoa for Bob and me while he looked for a Christmas movie on the small television in the kitchen. We were going to be up for a while since Ma had left more than a few presents to be wrapped. Bob found an old black and white movie starring Jimmy Stewart that neither of us had ever seen before, *It's A Wonderful Life*. It would become our favorite Christmas movie. I'm pretty sure the rest of the world followed our lead on that one.

Around three in the morning, we put the last of the gifts under the tree and turned off the lights. In the darkness, the tinsel sparkled and danced with the dim yellow light seeping in from the solitary street lamp outside. There were more presents crowded under the tree than I ever remembered. The kids weren't going to be disappointed this year when they woke up. Except for the fact that we were probably going to have to move soon, nothing had gone terribly wrong. I could finally enjoy Christmas.

The knee that hit me in the gut at six-thirty Christmas morning came from Danny landing on top of me. The one that got me in the head was from Erika. They both screamed, "Wake up! Santa came! And it's snowing!"

I didn't believe them, but when I looked out my bedroom window, there was at least eight inches of snow on the ground and still coming down hard. A back-door cold front had snuck into New England overnight and surprised everyone with what would ultimately accumulate to a foot of snow. It wasn't supposed to be, but there it was—a white Christmas.

The kids had a great morning opening gifts. Both Ma and Dad managed to get up to watch them. Janie even got her autographed picture of Lee Majors, although I doubt its authenticity to this day. I didn't get much in the way of presents, but it didn't matter. I had gotten what I really wanted—a good, maybe even great, Christmas for my brothers and sisters. And some snow.

Just before dinner, I went for a walk in the woods behind our apartment house. It was cold, and the sky was a deep, clear blue, silently succumbing to dusk. As I stood on the edge of the darkening woods looking out on a snow covered clearing, a cold emptiness suddenly took over. The only truly good Christmas I had ever known was almost gone. It would be forgotten tomorrow, and in a week, taken down and put away.

What was the point if this was how I felt at the end of the best Christmas in my young but worn life? Hadn't I been given what I really wanted?

No. I realized it wasn't true. I hadn't been given anything, not even the snow. I had given my brothers and sisters what they wanted. And in so doing, I had given myself my own Christmas wish.

I understood now. The cold emptiness would always be there. It was all those Christmases I never had—those Christmases that were supposed to be for me. They were gone. I would never have them. Christmas was now for someone else, for the people I cared most about, for my brothers and sisters ... for *my* eventual children ... for *my* future family.

With this revelation, I knew that Christmas would never disappoint me again, because I would never expect anything from it other than what I could control—what I gave to the people I loved. At fifteen, in the middle of a silent, dark, snow shrouded field, I determined that this was now what Christmas would always be for me.

When I returned from my walk, Christmas dinner was waiting with an apartment full of noise and kids and life. It was good—as good as I could ever remember.

Late that night, after everyone had left or gone to bed, I sat down and wrote this poem:

The Taking Down Of Christmas

The taking down of Christmas,
And putting love away,
And blowing out of candles,
To light another day.

Hibernate tree ornaments,
Leaving ice to fall,
While garland curls for winter sleep,
So naked, dead, and tall.

Cold clouds fall too late,
On a forgotten, lonely tree,
A wind of white dresses the night,
Freezing Christmas memories.

As through the white I wander,
Christmas Eve is here again,
Brothers, sisters decorate,
With dreams that fell from heaven.

A spilling forth of spirit,
We hope for Christmas white,
Children, eager, watch and wait,
Santa comes tonight.

The rising up for Christmas,
We know who early wake,
To peek at presents underneath,
Wrapped solely for their sake.

The passing fast of Christmas,
Let's sing a slow goodbye,
To love and life and family,
While lonely hearts still cry.

The rising morning solitude,
Christmas gone a year,
Though spirit lingers on in us,
The time has left to share.

A drifted porch glows in the night,
With snow that cannot last,
As ending now my walk of white,
And thoughts of Christmas past.

The rain has come, the snow is done,
I'm warm but cold inside,
'til children's voices full of joy,
Shout Christmas has not died.

The taking down of Christmas,
And leaving love to stay,
And letting candles warm my house,
Not just on Christmas day.

And though the light of humanity flickers,
Uncertain to last the darkening years,
A breath from each, his own candle,
Brightens with each Christmas cheer.

The Ninth Child

BIG MEMORIES
IN LITTLE BOXES

When I sat down to write about my favorite Christmas memory, I couldn't. It's not because I don't have any or the ones I have aren't good. It's because there isn't one big Christmas memory that dominates everything else. Yes, there are bad ones. How could there not be with the way we grew up. But I remember many small good ones even more.

Like some of the cheap, two-dollar toys we got as presents every Christmas—sometimes the only things we got—that we somehow turned into hours and hours of fun. And those ugly clothes Ma would pick out for us girls that never fit and were nowhere close to what we wanted. Ma definitely favored the boys. They always got one pair of socks each, all the same size. Now we all laugh at each other's stories of those awful Christmas clothes when we get together for a family event.

Then there was the competition every Christmas Eve to see who could find the biggest and best old sock to use as a stocking, as if that would make a difference in what Santa put in them. We always had a lot of unmatched socks because we never had enough of them to be able to throw away a pair when one wore out. All those mismatched socks we wore would be chic today. We usually taped our stockings on a kitchen chair Christmas Eve, sometimes a window sill. There was that one year that Bobby and Billy built a cardboard fireplace for Erika and Danny. We tried to hang the stockings on it but it tipped over. I think they ended up nailing the fake fireplace to the wall and getting in trouble for it.

And I remember that year in Amesbury when we got a surprise white Christmas, and we all went tobogganing in the dark down Poplar Street where we lived. It was a really steep street but deserted because we lived right across from an abandoned factory. There were like eight or nine of us on the toboggan. Someone had a flashlight so we could see where we were going, which was ridiculous because there was no way we could steer the toboggan with so many people on it. Kevin, Billy and Bobby pushed it to get us going really fast and then jumped on top of the pile. We smashed into a snow bank the first time and everyone went flying. It was so much fun, we ran back up the hill to do it again. Eventually, someone got hurt—me, but I rallied back. That became a tradition whenever it snowed.

Some of my favorite memories are the decorating and singing we would do every Christmas Eve before going to bed. It was always chaotic and crazy, or that's how it seemed to me. Sometimes, we argued and fought, but most of the time I remember everyone laughing. I looked forward to that night every year.

Oh, I can't forget to mention Mr. Richardson, the owner of the local package store where Ma and Dad bought their beer and cigarettes. After we moved back to the same drug infested street in Beverly that we had been kicked out of three and a half years earlier, he started coming by every Christmas to give Ma some money to buy presents for us kids. I'm sure he knew what was going on and wanted to help. I think we actually started to expect him to come every year, almost like Santa Claus.

The anticipation every Christmas morning when I woke up was unbearable, but we managed to keep ourselves busy while we waited. We were good at that. It always seemed to be cold too. I remember how we would all huddle around the heating grate in the bathroom waiting for Ma to finally wake up and give the go ahead to open our presents. There was always disappointment, but the excitement as we shivered and laughed and waited together is one of my favorite memories of my life.

I could go on and on, but that's why I couldn't come up with just one memory to write about. Christmas growing up for me is a series of small, special memories. I don't dwell on the disappointment. I remember all those little Christmas scenes instead, like tiny miracles scattered about in our hard lives. I think they're the most enduring gift of all, and the gift I want to share with whoever reads this. So, when I finally stopped trying to come up with one special story, I got the inspiration for this poem:

MY CHRISTMAS MEMORIES

'Twas the night before Christmas in the Cunningham house,
Dad was asleep, passed out on the couch,
Our socks were all taped on a kitchen chair,
I hoped that Santa would know they were there,
We were all lying down, three to a bed,
All the toys that I wanted dancing in my head,
Ma in her lipstick, some kid on her lap,
Taking a rest, then some gifts she would wrap,
When out in the kitchen, I heard such a clatter,
We all ran out to see what was the matter,
I thought it was Santa, but I guess I was wrong,
Boy, the night before Christmas was always so long,
I looked out the window—Could Santa be here?
It was just Mr. Richardson, the guy who sold beer,
I remember the times of new fallen snow,
The lights on the tree, oh how they did glow,
The memories I have, I think of once in a while,
I kept all the good ones, the rest are on file,
Playing games in the kitchen is what I recall,
Parcheesi, Battling Tops and Nerf basketball,
The songs we would sing with our terrible voices,
Watching Rudolph and Frosty were always good choices,
Making our red and green Christmas Rings,
Having each other was a wonderful thing,
Than waiting for Santa to come to our house,
A sleigh full of toys and some ugly new blouse,
The Christmases we shared throughout all the years,
Some made me happy, and some brought me tears,

So as I think back on when I was a kid,
I try to remember some had even less than we did,
Now that most of us have children, many of them grown,
We give them the best present—great memories of their own,
I think of you all as I turn out the light,
Merry Christmas to all and to all a good night!

The Tenth Child

JAILHOUSE ANGELS

The officer on night duty told me I could be released tomorrow, Christmas Eve, if I could make bail. I remember his name was Pete. I had already gotten to know him. He was a good guy, big and fat. He had played football and baseball for Lynn English High School and was only a few years older than me. We knew a lot of the same guys from North Shore high school sports. He thought he knew something about the Red Sox and Bruins too. He didn't know anything, but I had to pretend like he did since he could decide to be either Santa or the Abominable Snowman in dealing with me.

I guess this isn't technically about my favorite Christmas memory. Hanging out in a small holding cell at the Lynn Police Department the night before Christmas Eve wasn't exactly a special Yuletide experience for me. But it's one of my best Christmas memories and an awesome story! I love telling it!

It's 1985, and I'm twenty. No need to go into why I was in a holding cell trying to make bail. Suffice it to say, I was arrested for another stupid thing I did, but it wasn't anything serious. The problem was that I had a bunch of unpaid parking tickets too that I didn't have the money to pay. On top of that, I still owed a local law firm money for representing me in a previous stupid incident. Because of that, no lawyer in the area who worked on cases like mine would do anything for me until I paid off my old bills to the other lawyer. It's a sleazy little code they follow to make sure they all get paid.

Since Christmas Eve was the next day, there was a pretty good chance I wouldn't be able to get a public defender to represent me either. I was looking at spending Christmas in a six by eight-foot cell, without decorations or a fireplace.

Three walls of my cell were all cement painted a dull white. The fourth was cement too, but it faced the hallway and had a metal door with a small square window of bars in it. There was a narrow, horizontal opening at the bottom of the window to pass things through like meal trays. The ceiling was so low that I felt like I needed to hunch every time I stood up. I made a joke to Pete that if I had to stay there through Christmas, I would get Santa Claustrophobic. It took him a second to get it.

Anyway, I called my older brother Billy who had a job with a consulting firm in Boston. I remembered him telling me he was making almost $30,000 a year, which seemed huge at the time. I assumed it was because he graduated from an Ivy League college. He had just moved to an apartment in Boston with my other brother Bobby. They're twins. I left a message on their phone machine asking Billy if he would put up my bail so I could get out before Christmas.

I wasn't sure how Billy would respond since I still owed him $500 that he'd lent me last year for a down payment on a used car. It turned out I couldn't really afford the payments, so it was repossessed after six months. It was a crappy car anyways. The dealer ripped me off, but I was a sucker too. I should have shopped around more.

There were seven holding cells, all in a row. Five of them were occupied, one guy to a cell. I was in the middle one with two guys on either side of me. The cell on either end was empty. I joked with Pete that it was cozy, just like growing up sleeping in a twin bed with my oldest and youngest brothers. He didn't have much of a sense of humor. Or maybe he didn't care.

The guy farthest to my left was named Dick. I remember his name because we all made a lot of prison jokes at his expense when he told us. He was an old white guy and a drunk. He said he spent three or four nights there a month. More during the cold weather.

Chuck was the guy immediately to my left. He was in his twenties and had gotten into a fight at some bar. When the cops showed up, he gave them some lip. Lynn police didn't take lip from anyone. Chuck was a small guy and nasty, with something to prove.

I figured out that the two guys on my right were both black. I told Pete it was segregation, and I was going to call Judge Garrity as soon as I got out. He didn't get the joke again. Neither of the black guys had a clue who I was talking about either. So, I explained that Garrity was the judge who forced bussing on South Boston where I was born. That got James, the black guy in the cell just to my right, going for a little while.

James was eighteen, a big talker and a dropout from Lynn Tech, the vocational high school. From what I could tell, he was a tall, skinny kid since he complained about having to bend over when he stood up. And his arm was really long and thin when he stuck it through the bars to wave to me. He said he was there because the police made a mistake thinking he was trying to break into a car, but he was just admiring it. He was either stupid or young to try to get away with that defense. I guessed both.

The black guy farthest to my right was Mohamed. From what he said, he seemed about thirty. I remember he was a sharp guy and suspicious of everyone. I asked him why he was there. He told me it was none of my business. I did get him talking enough to learn that his real name was Ray and that he had adopted Mohamed when he converted to Muslim last year. I later got Pete to tell me Ray was arrested for drug dealing, his second time.

A drunk, a punk, a thief, a dealer, and me—five wise guys all together the night before Christmas Eve. If I was going to be stuck there with them, I was going to have some fun. So, after our meager dinners, I got everyone except Dick shouting and arguing back and forth about whether the Celtics or Lakers were better.

James, the black kid on my right, must have played basketball because he was adamant that the Lakers were superior and that Magic Johnson would beat Larry Bird in a one-on-one match. Even though he was black, Ray liked Bird and got into it with James. Chuck let us know he was a hockey fan and hated basketball, but he threw his two cents behind the Lakers anyway because he liked arguing. We were all sticking our arms out as far as we could through the bars, waving high fives in the air, clenching our fists and giving each other the finger over various points and counterpoints. In the middle of it all, I started

82

shouting, "AttiChristmas! AttiChristmas! AttiChristmas!" It was hysterical.

Then Dick starts kicking his cell door like a lunatic and yelling that he has to get out of there right now so he can buy his son the baseball glove he promised him for Christmas. Everyone stopped arguing and tried to look down towards his cell. The idea that Dick had a kid was unbelievable, even though we had only known each other four hours. We all assumed he was just an old, homeless drunk.

Suddenly, everything was quiet. So, Chuck shouts, "You ain't got no kid, old man. If ya did, he'd be a hundred years old and—"

"What's all the noise in here?" Pete boomed, interrupting Chuck as he swung open the heavy metal door to the hallway.

I could see Dick in the small, round mirror up in the corner at the end of the hallway. His face was pushed up against the bars on his cell window and his left hand stuck out like he was reaching for Pete. "Officer, officer, I have to get out of here," Dick begged. "It's my son's birthday. I promised to buy him a new baseball glove. Please, let me out."

Pete walked down to Dick's window and said, "It's okay, Richard. Your son's birthday is tomorrow, remember? We'll let you out then. You'll have plenty of time to get him that glove. Now try to get some sleep."

"Tomorrow?" Dick said. "Oh yeah, it's tomorrow … okay … but you'll let me out, right?"

"Like always, Richard," Pete replied and started to walk back towards the door.

Then Chuck quipped, "See, I told you he's too old to have a kid."

"Hey! Shut it!" Pete snapped at Chuck. "His son was a war hero. He died in Vietnam saving a bunch of men and got the *Medal of Honor* for it. We look out for him. You get what I'm saying? And his son's birthday *is* tomorrow. Show some respect."

Chuck remembered what happened to him when he gave a Lynn cop some lip earlier that day and quickly shut up. Pete walked out and let the door slam behind him like he was making a point. It was quiet for a few seconds and then I shouted, "Hey Dick, so your son liked baseball? I played a lot myself growing up. What position did he play?"

"He's a pitcher," Dick answered clearly.

"I was a pitcher, too," I said. "Could he hit?"

"He has a great bat," Dick answered.

"I pitched a little and played shortstop," Ray interjected.

James added, "I always played first base because I was tall and a lefty, but I quit to play basketball. I sucked at hitting."

Then Chuck piped in, "I was a catcher. I had a rifle for an arm. I would have been drafted if I had stuck with it."

James, Ray and I booed and laughed at Chuck's bragging. He got angry and started to swear at us when Dick said something. We stopped shouting and I asked, "What was that, Dick?"

"I believe you, Chuck," Dick said.

We all shut up. Then Chuck said, "Thanks. Tell your son happy birthday for me."

"Oh, that's right, his birthday's tomorrow, Christmas Eve ... I read him *The Night Before Christmas* and sing him songs before he goes to bed ... uh, what was I saying?"

"You sing your son Christmas songs before he goes to bed," I answered.

"Oh yeah ... but I can't remember any," Dick said. "Anyone know any Christmas songs?"

"I know most of *Rudolph*, maybe some of *Frosty*," Chuck replied.

"I can whistle *Jingle Bells*," James offered, "but I don't know many of the words."

"I'm Muslim," Ray added. "We don't sing."

"You came to the right jail, Dick," I shouted. "I have older twin brothers who always sang Christmas carols to me and my younger brother and sister growing up. They had awful voices, but it always got us in the Christmas spirit."

Just then, Pete opened the hallway door and shouted, "Thirty minutes to lights out."

After the door closed, Dick asked, "Did someone say he knows some Christmas songs?"

"Yeah, I did. It's Sean," I shouted.

"Sean, can you tell me the words to a couple of them ... and hum the tune?" Dick asked.

"I don't wanna hear no white guy humming," James shouted and laughed.

"Me neither," Chuck added. "Let Ray or James do the humming."

"I'm Muslim," Ray said. "We don't hum."

Dick started to get worked up and said, "Sean, I need Christmas songs for my son …"

"I got you covered, Dick," I shouted. "I know a million songs, and I have a great voice too. Don't listen to these guys. They're just jealous."

"Can you sing them?" Dick asked eagerly.

"I got an even better idea," I said. "I'll tell everyone the words first and then start singing so you pick up the tune. Then you can all join in. Hey, if we're going to be stuck here for Christmas, then we should make the best of it and get in the holiday spirit."

"I'd like that, Sean," Dick said, calmer now.

"I guess no one will hear me make an ass of myself in here," Chuck yelled. "Count me in."

"Hey man, I'll try too," James offered, sticking his long arm and hand out between the bars on his cell window and pointing his thumb up.

"I'm Muslim—" Ray started.

"Yeah, yeah, you don't sing or hum," I interrupted him. "Muslims chant, don't they? Just chant along, okay? For Dick."

Ray didn't respond, and I didn't wait. I announced that we were starting with *Rudolph the Red Nosed Reindeer*. It was a little rough at the start, with me doing the brunt of the singing and projecting, but by the third song, *A Holly Jolly Christmas*, Chuck and James were belting the versus as loud as they could, adding different twists to the words, sometimes crude and sometimes obscene, but always funny. I heard Ray laugh loudly a few times too.

During *Frosty the Snowman*, I started to hear special effects noises and humming coming from Ray's cell. When we were about to begin *Hark! The Herald Angels Sing*, Ray stopped us and said, "I'm not going to let you guys mutilate this song like the others. I'll lead … and James, you can't be a brother with that voice."

James replied, "Hey bro, I'm only eighteen. My voice is still changing, alright?"

"Why do you like this song, Ray? Were you a choir boy?" Chuck shouted and laughed.

"Maybe I was, but this choir boy can kick your ass," Ray shot back.

"Whoa there, angels," I shouted. "Peace on Earth and all that crap. I think we might have the start of a rock group here—*The Jailhouse Angels*. Let's keep going. Ray, you got the mike."

Ray didn't say anything for a while. Then Dick asked, "Could someone sing that song, please? I used to sing it to my son when he was young, before he died … I don't remember the words anymore."

"I got it," Ray shouted before anyone could respond. Ray led us in that song and several other classic Christmas carols. He knew every verse, and he had a pretty good voice, for a drug dealer … and a Muslim who didn't sing or hum.

Pete walked in a few minutes before lights out and said, "I didn't really hear you guys singing Christmas carols, did I?"

"Hell no," Chuck answered, "but you got some pretty talented rats in this place."

"Big rats," James added, and we all laughed.

"You have a favorite Christmas song, Pete?" I asked.

"*Little Drummer Boy*," Pete answered.

"I love that one too," I said, then shouted, "Hey Dick, you okay if we finish off with *The Little Drummer Boy*?"

"That's good. Thank you, Sean," Dick answered.

I started and then everyone joined in, even Pete. The song echoed down the hall of cells, making our voices sound almost holy, like we were in a cathedral. I know I sound like a stereotype, but it really was wicked cool.

After we finished, everyone said Merry Christmas to each other, although Ray reminded us again that he was Muslim. Pete left and the lights dimmed. As I lay there in my bunk staring at the graffiti on the ceiling, I heard someone singing *Silent Night*. It was an awesome voice, and I'm pretty sure it was coming from Dick's cell. *Silent Night* was always the last song we used to sing on Christmas Eve growing up. My spine tingled as I fell asleep.

Billy came and bailed me out early Christmas Eve morning. I never said goodbye to any of *The Jailhouse Angels* and never heard about any of them again.

When Billy asked me how it was spending the night in jail, I said, "It sucked, although some of it was fun. Kind of like growing up … but I don't want to do either one again."

The Eleventh Child

I STILL BELIEVE IN SANTA

There comes a point in every kid's life when he questions if Santa Claus is real. It happened to me the summer after I turned ten years old. July 5, 1979, to be exact. I remember because it was the morning after the apartment building we lived in caught on fire. It was a run-down triple-decker in Beverly. We didn't have much, but what little we did have was destroyed by the fire and the water damage from putting it out, including my new baseball glove.

I still remember waking up just before midnight on July 4th to my older sister Janie screaming, "Fire! Ma, the apartment's on fire!" Then my older brother Billy came running into the bedroom where I was sleeping with my brother, Sean. Billy was carrying my younger sister, Erika. He rushed all of us out to the sidewalk on the other side of the street where my mother was standing with Janie and my sister Debbie. Then he went back inside with my Dad to make sure everyone was out. They came back and said they couldn't get upstairs to check the second or third floor apartments because the smoke and flames were too much.

Erika started crying and asked where Bobby was. He's Billy's twin. I tried to be strong, but I started to cry too. Billy said Bobby was at his girlfriend's and then reassured us that everything would be okay. I remember asking him about my baseball glove. It was all I could think about at the time, probably because I was in shock. I don't remember what he said. Then the fire trucks showed up, and he and Debbie put Sean, Erika, and me in his car and drove us to my sister Cathy's apartment a few streets away to get us away from all the craziness.

We slept in Cathy's apartment that night. I woke up early and went to the kitchen where Billy and Bobby were talking to Cathy. I asked where Ma was, and Bobby told me she was at our apartment trying to salvage some things. I learned a few years later that she had actually refused to leave after the fire was put out. She sat on a chair in the driveway all night smoking and drinking. The fire was just another crisis for her to thrive on.

I asked Bobby how Ma could save anything from the fire. He said the firemen had been able to put out the fire before it destroyed our apartment building and that it was safe now to grab any of our stuff that we could. I asked him if he could get my baseball glove. He said he would try when he went to pick up Ma. But when Bobby returned with Ma, he said almost everything was destroyed and the firemen made him leave before he could look for it because the ceiling was about to collapse from all the water on the second floor.

I started to cry. That's when Ma said that Santa would bring me a new one for Christmas. My eyes lit up and I wiped my tears away. But I was ten years old, and by that time, I had heard a lot of rumors from other kids who said Santa wasn't real. Even before the fire, I had worried that it was true. Now I was afraid that if Santa didn't exist, I wouldn't get a new glove.

Billy saw the look on my face and said, "Don't worry, Danny. We can get you a new glove this week."

I said, "Really? Okay."

But things got worse the rest of that summer. We didn't have a place to live, so most of us ended up sleeping at my sister Cathy's apartment, at least at first. It was small, with only two bedrooms. She was married with two kids herself. There wasn't room for Billy and Bobby, so they slept in their old Impala parked in the driveway of Cathy's apartment building. Ma and Dad used the crisis as an excuse to drink every day late into the night at Cathy's, which led to arguments with Cathy's husband, especially over money since Ma and Dad blew what they had on beer and cigarettes and didn't help out. Cathy's husband kicked them out, and we all left, except Billy and Bobby, who kept sleeping in their car. Ma and Dad managed to find a one bedroom apartment for a few weeks and then a two bedroom apartment after that. I never did get my glove.

At the end of the summer, Billy and Bobby headed off to college—Billy to Brown and Bobby to Dartmouth. They were the first in the family to ever go away to college. It was hard on Erika and me when they left because they had been mostly taking care of us since I could remember. Then Debbie moved out to get married and have a baby. Now, it was just Janie, Sean, Erika and me left, with Rebel, our big mutt of a dog. We survived like we always did.

Around Thanksgiving, Ma and Dad found another apartment in Beverly, and we moved again. This time it was pretty decent. It had four bedrooms on a much safer street. Things were getting a little better. We didn't know how long it would last, but then again, we never did.

As Christmas approached, I started to hope for a new baseball glove from Santa. But I was even more anxious now because some kids at school were teasing anyone who talked about Santa like he was real. When I asked my older brothers and sisters if Santa existed, they all said the same thing—he was real. In my own mind, though, I still wasn't sure.

It was about a week before Christmas and I was sitting on the floor watching a Bruins game. Dad was sitting in his chair watching with me, drinking a beer and smoking a cigarette. Ma was in the kitchen talking on the phone with Nana, her mother. During a commercial, I turned to Dad and asked, "Do you believe in Santa?"

I remember Dad's answer like it was yesterday because it was the start of some special memories no one else in my family has. It was also the start of me really growing up.

Dad smirked at me and said, "I'm going to see Santa tomorrow. Wanna come?"

I didn't know what to say. Dad kidded with us a lot when he drank, so I was skeptical. I said, "What do mean?"

Dad said, "I'm taking a trip tomorrow to pick up some toys from Mr. Claus' Warehouse in Detroit. If you wanna find out if Santa is real, you can come with me."

Dad was a truck driver and sometimes went on long haul road trips for several days to other parts of the country.

I said, "How come you have to pick up Santa's toys?"

Dad said, "They're probably just extra."

I thought for a moment and then asked, "You really going to where Santa Claus keeps extra toys?"

Dad took a puff of his cigarette, smirked again and said, "You'll have to come with me to find out."

I said, "But I can't miss school."

Dad said, "Have it your way, Danny, but how many kids get to go on a trip with their old man to find out if Santa's real?"

I got up from the floor and said I was going to ask Ma if it was okay. I went into the kitchen, but Ma was still talking to Nana on the phone. When I went back to tell Dad I had to wait to ask Ma, he was falling asleep in his chair. I sat down and finished watching the game. I decided Dad was just playing with me.

But Dad woke me up early the next morning and told me to get dressed and pack an extra pair of underwear if I wanted to go with him.

I asked, "Did Ma say it was okay?"

Dad said, "Do you wanna come or not?"

I was excited but nervous as I drove with Dad to his work to pick up his tractor-trailer. I remember climbing up for the first time to the passenger seat in the cab of the tractor. It was high off the ground, and there were a lot of gear sticks. I felt powerful. It was really cool.

Dad grabbed a cup of coffee and a donut out of a machine for himself and a chocolate candy bar for me before we hit the road in the 18-wheeler. The sun was just coming up behind us as Dad turned onto the Mass Pike headed west for Detroit and Mr. Claus' Warehouse.

I remember falling asleep as the big rig rambled on and on. It felt like we hit every pothole and bump in the road. I woke up a little while later and said I had to go to the bathroom. Dad told me that I had to learn how to hold it in if I was going to be a truck driver some day. It was painful trying not to wet my pants. Finally, Dad pulled into a truck stop with a diner somewhere in New York State.

I had pancakes for lunch and Dad had a roast beef sandwich. A lot of people at the diner came over to talk to Dad and say "hi" to me.

One waitress made a particular big deal over me. I remember she had really strong smelling perfume. Dad was obviously a regular. I learned later that he always made that his first stop on long hauls west and his last stop coming back.

That first day driving was really boring. The road just went on and on, with some hills and some turns and some straightaways over and over again. Dad smoked five or six cigarettes every hour. When the ashtray got filled up, he'd finish a cigarette, roll down his window, and flick the butt outside. The lit ashes would explode when they hit the air rushing by at sixty miles an hour. Then Dad would light up a new cigarette two minutes later.

Dad stared at the road with incredible concentration for hours without saying anything while we listened to country and western music on the radio. I tried to copy him but I quickly gave up. Every now and then, he'd turn the radio down and point out something like a hawk in the sky or an old car on the road or a barn in a corn field and tell me a short story about growing up on a farm outside of Detroit. Sometimes something would remind him of when he was in the Navy during the Korean War and I would get to hear about that. I never thought of Dad as very talkative, but he had a lot of little stories.

Dad taught me how to pump gas into an 18-wheeler on that trip. He also showed me how to talk to a State Trooper when you got pulled over for speeding. He managed to let the Trooper know I was riding in the cab with him and that he was trying to get me home in time to make it to school the next day. Even though I was only ten, I got the joke and stared at the Trooper with my blue eyes and managed a meek smile. I don't remember if the Trooper let him off that time, but it definitely worked a few times on later trips I took with Dad.

It had been dark for a while when we pulled into an all night diner and truck stop. Dad told me we were staying there for the night and that we'd sleep in the bunk behind the seats in the tractor cab. After we sat down and ordered something to eat, he left to use the pay phone to check in with his work. When he returned, he told me he had called Ma and that she was mad at him and me. I didn't know why I was in trouble too. I said Friday was a half day and that I was really only missing three days of school.

Dad said, "She'll get over it. You'll learn more on this trip than an entire year of school. Even your mother will admit that."

Then our food arrived and Dad ordered another beer. I think I had pancakes again.

It was cold sleeping in the tractor that night. I remember having strange dreams. Dad snored a lot, probably because he had gotten a little drunk. But he woke up early, and we hit the road before sunrise. We both had English muffins for breakfast that we ate in the tractor. Dad shared a little of his coffee with me. I was wide awake for the rest of the trip to Detroit.

We arrived at Mr. Claus' Warehouse on the outskirts of Detroit early in the afternoon. It was a big storage facility with a small store in front that displayed all sorts of Christmas themed toys and decorations. It would probably seem cheap to me now, but back then it was amazing. Dad told me to hang out inside the store while he backed into the loading dock to pick up the freight he was hauling back to Boston.

I walked around checking everything out while I looked for anyone who might be Santa. I peeked through the door to the warehouse floor and saw Dad talking to a big, fat guy with a full beard. He looked too young to be Santa, and his beard was dark brown. I thought he might be Santa in disguise.

After about an hour, Dad came and got me. We walked across the warehouse floor to his truck. The big guy with the beard was standing there writing something on a clipboard. Dad took a piece of paper from the guy and then said to me that we were leaving.

I said, "But I thought we were going to meet Santa?"

Dad looked at me funny like he didn't know what I was talking about. Then he seemed to understand. He looked up at the big guy with the beard and smiled. The big guy smiled back at Dad. Then the guy looked down at me and said, "I'm not Santa, if that's what you think. Santa was here earlier but had to go back to the North Pole to get ready for Christmas."

Dad smirked and looked down at me. He said, "Satisfied? Let's go."

I wasn't satisfied, but what was I going to say? I climbed into the tractor, and Dad took off with a truck full of extra toys from Santa.

Dad didn't say anything for an hour. When he finally did talk, he said that we were going to Cleveland and then Pittsburgh to drop off some of the freight before heading back to Boston.

We parked at a truck stop just outside of Cleveland because it was too late to deliver anything. We ate McDonalds in the cab and then climbed in back to sleep. Before I fell asleep, Dad said, "Danny, I know you wanted to see Santa, but you're old enough now to know you don't always get what you want."

I said, "But you said I was going to see Santa for real."

Dad said, "Come on, you're seeing things your friends won't believe."

I didn't say anything back. I remember quietly crying myself to sleep thinking Dad had lied to me. It wasn't the first time, but this time hurt a lot. When I woke up, I told myself that I wasn't going to stop believing in Santa just because he wasn't in Detroit.

The weather was pretty bad that day. It was raining and sleeting all the way to Pittsburgh. Dad didn't talk much because he was focused on the road. He didn't even listen to the radio. It made me nervous, but every now and then Dad would say something funny to me and I'd feel better.

The weather cleared and turned very cold by the time we pulled into the same diner again in New York. It was dinner time. I ordered pancakes from the waitress with the strong perfume. I don't remember what Dad ate. All I remember is him getting pretty drunk before bringing me to the truck and telling me to go to sleep. Then he went back inside.

I lay awake waiting for Dad to return for what seemed like hours. I eventually fell asleep but woke up when he finally did climb into the bunk. He smelled of beer and the same strong perfume that the waitress did. I remember it took me a while to fall back asleep, especially once Dad started to snore. To this day, I don't think anything really happened that night, but I grew up a lot that trip. I would see a lot more on other trips, and grow up a lot more too.

When I woke up the next morning, it was even more important to me to believe that Santa was real. I was determined to figure it out for myself, but I wasn't sure how. Then it came to me. I'd stay up all night

Christmas Eve until it was morning and see if Santa showed up for myself. I had tried it before but always fell asleep. After this road trip, I knew I was big enough to do it.

Dad made it back to Boston by noon, dropped off the rest of his freight at a place in South Boston near the water, and then drove back to his work. We got home just before dark. I thought Ma would yell at us when we walked in the door, but she just smiled and asked me what I thought of the trip. I realized she was pretty drunk already. Then Janie, Erika, and Sean came from the kitchen to greet me. I smelled spaghetti cooking. I was happy to be home.

The next night was the night before Christmas Eve. We still didn't have our tree. Billy and Bobby had gotten the tree the past several years, but Erika, Sean and I didn't know what to expect with them being away at college. They were supposed to be home for their Christmas vacation earlier that day, but they hadn't arrived yet. When I asked Dad if we were going to get a tree, he said maybe tomorrow.

Janie heard him and yelled, "We're not getting a Christmas tree! Ma, Dad's not going to buy a tree!"

Dad got mad and yelled at Janie and then Ma got mad and yelled at him. They were both a little drunk. Sean spoke up and said, "Dad, I'll get the tree if you give me the money."

Sean was fourteen and trying to do some of the parenting things Billy and Bobby used to do. I wanted to be grown up like him and said I'd help. Then Erika offered to help too. Janie calmed down and asked if she could help as well.

Dad looked up from his chair at Sean and said, "You wanna get the tree?" Then he took twenty dollars out of his pocket and threw it on the coffee table in front of him. He added, "Bring me back some change."

Sean grabbed the money before Dad could change his mind. Then we all put our coats on and headed off to the parking lot about a half mile away where they were selling Christmas trees.

Janie didn't have good eyesight but she was the one who found the best tree. The problem was it cost twenty-five dollars. The guy selling them knew Sean and asked how much money he had. Sean said fifteen bucks. The guy said he would sell it to us for twenty if we got another five. Sean pulled out the twenty Dad had given him. The guy laughed, and we had our tree.

Trying to carry a big Christmas tree a half mile home wasn't so easy for a fourteen-year-old, a ten-year-old, a seven-year-old, and Janie. I wanted to show that I was grown up and strong enough to carry one end by myself, but the tree was too big. We had to drag it along the sidewalk. It was cold, and Janie was the only one who had gloves. Some branches broke, and we started arguing out of frustration. Then Erika began to cry. That's when a big car pulled up next to us. It was Billy and Bobby in their Impala!

They tied the tree on the roof of their car, and we all climbed in. I insisted on helping carry the tree into our apartment and setting it in the stand. I also helped put the lights and garland on. I wanted to show Billy and Bobby that I was grown up now.

Christmas Eve was finally here. I was still worried about getting a new glove, but I was more worried about something else. With Billy and Bobby off at college, I had started to think I should take on some of the responsibilities they used to do. Going on the road trip with Dad had convinced me I was ready to step up. But something didn't feel right. How could I be grown up if I still believed in Santa Claus?

I was determined to find out if Santa really existed. So I told Billy and Bobby I was staying up all night to see for myself if Santa was real. I think they understood what was going on, or else they didn't think I could stay awake that late. Either way, they said it was up to me. That made me feel big.

Billy and Bobby still wanted to sing Christmas songs to Erika, Sean and me like they used to before they left for college. Sean didn't join in, but he listened while Erika and I sang with them. We all joke about their singing now, but it was one of my favorite parts of Christmas. After they were done and tucking us into bed, I said to Bobby quietly so Erika couldn't hear, "Should I still believe in Santa Claus? A lot of my friends don't."

Bobby smiled and then leaned over and whispered, "Everyone needs to believe in something good. It can be Santa or anything you want. Decide for yourself and don't listen to anyone who tries to tell you not to believe. That's being grown up. Now, get some sleep so Santa can come."

I said, "But I'm staying awake, remember?"

He nodded and said, "Sorry, I forgot. Well, pretend right now so Erika falls asleep. Okay?"

Erika usually slept in her own bed in another bedroom with Janie, but tonight she was sleeping in my bed because it was Christmas Eve and she didn't want to be by herself. I nodded to Bobby and closed my eyes. Erika fell asleep right away, but I lay in bed with my mind stirring with all these different thoughts about Santa. Was he real? Will he know I'm watching for him? How will he come down the chimney if we don't have one, not even a cardboard one like that year that we built one?

I could hear the low sound of the radio playing Christmas carols in the kitchen where Billy and Bobby were still up wrapping the presents they had bought. One of them would check on us every now and then. I would fake being asleep.

To help stay awake, I kept climbing out of bed to look out the window to see if I could catch a glimpse of Santa and his reindeer, maybe even Rudolf. I even snuck out to the front room once to peek at the Christmas tree for presents to make sure Santa hadn't come yet.

As the night went on and I didn't hear or see anything, I started to get discouraged. I finally fell asleep with tears in my eyes because Santa and his reindeer hadn't shown up. It was all just make believe.

Suddenly, I woke up to a loud noise and some weird sounds! I sat up and listened. Everything was quiet. Erika was still sleeping, and Sean was in his bed with his back to me. The kitchen light was off, which meant everyone had gone to bed. Then I saw a big red light pass by quickly outside my window, and I heard, "Ho! Ho! Ho! Merry Christmas!"

I stared at the window, but the red light was already gone. Then I heard sleigh bells ring really loud. When the ringing started to fade, I jumped out of bed and ran to look out my window, but Santa was no longer there. I turned and ran to the front room. Santa had left presents all around our Christmas tree! Then I ran to Billy and Bobby's room. They were sitting on their beds wide awake and still dressed for some reason. I told them how Santa is real and how I saw Rudolph pass by my window. They acted almost as excited as me.

I didn't think I could but I fell back to sleep pretty quickly after that. Erika woke up first Christmas morning, and we snuck out to the front room to look at all the presents under the tree. A plate with some cookie crumbs on it and a half empty glass of milk were on the coffee table next to a note from Santa. I remember it said at the end: "P.S., always believe in me!"

After a little while, we woke up Billy and Bobby so we could open our presents. They made us some cocoa while we waited for Ma and Dad to get up. Dad kept sleeping, but when Ma got up, we dove into the presents.

Even after hearing Santa and seeing Rudolph's red nose, I was still nervous as I opened my presents. Then I found it! It felt a little soft and had different wrapping from a lot of the other presents I got. I tore the paper off and saw my new baseball glove!

By the next Christmas, I had been on a few more road trips with Dad and grown up a lot more. I had mostly figured out what was going on with Santa too, but I had also figured out how to believe in him without worrying about what other kids thought. You had to believe in something good to survive the way we all grew up. When I was little, it was Santa. As I got older, it changed to whatever got me through the new family crisis I had no control over. But when I look back, I realize it was all just hope in different forms.

And that's why I still believe in Santa Claus, even now that I am grown up.

The Twelfth Child

THE TWELVE CHILDREN
OF CHRISTMAS

My family loves to sing. Most of us will readily admit we're not very good at it, but that confession is usually about some other sibling's voice, not our own. Some of us could probably have been good singers since we were all pretty creative and talented. But growing up in a large family with little money, singing lessons would have ranked somewhere around 459th on the list of spending priorities, right after a pet Llama, had there been a list, or any extra money after cigarettes, beer, food, rent and the frequent unpaid utility bill.

When I think about it, though, it's kind of funny that none of us ever ended up pursuing something musical in our lives. Ma and Dad both loved music and musicals. As an escape during the Depression, Ma spent much of her teenage years in movie theaters watching every film she could, and musicals were her favorite. Dad also loved musicals and would often make us sit down in front of the television to watch some classic that we had never heard of and had no interest in seeing. Halfway through, he would tell us we could leave if we wanted to. By that time, of course, we were too engrossed and would finish watching the musical, much to his satisfaction.

Despite our lack of musical training, we still had plenty of fun singing, especially during the holidays. We sang Easter songs, Fourth of July songs, Halloween songs and songs for Thanksgiving. But it was Christmas time when we sang the most. If we weren't singing, we were listening to Christmas songs on the radio or playing the one Christmas album we had—*Rudolph the Red-Nosed Reindeer*—nonstop for hours at a time. At night when we would go to bed, my older brothers, Billy and Bobby, would sing us younger kids to sleep with Christmas songs. Actually, they would more often than not sing us awake since we would be so wound up after their animated performances that it would take us another hour to fall asleep. It was a ton of fun and a very special time for all of us.

The first Christmas that I have any memory of is when I was about two-and-a-half years old. That's the year we first recorded our family rendition of *The Twelve Days of Christmas*. Although a lot of the details of that Christmas have been filled in for me over the years by my older brothers and sisters, it is the story I want to tell here because it was the start of a special Cunningham family tradition that has given me my best Christmas memories.

It was Christmas night at our apartment in Amesbury. My oldest sister Gale, her husband Bob, and their two boys, Michael and Shane, were visiting, along with my sister Cathy, her husband, and their son Billy. Michael and Billy were older than me even though I was their aunt. That's what happens when you're the last of twelve kids—you get lapped by the children of your oldest siblings.

Ma and Dad were already well on the other side of tipsy. My two brothers-in-law were arguing with Dad about sports, while Ma was debating something about President Nixon with my older sister Gale. Billy and Bobby were keeping all of the younger kids occupied by organizing games of tag, hide-and-go-seek, and *Capture the Reindeer*— their own invention. All together, there were eighteen of us celebrating Christmas in a three-bedroom apartment. It was loud, boisterous, smoky, and crowded. And for me—a wide-eyed, precocious two-and-a-half year old girl—it was wonderful!

In the middle of all of this chaos, my oldest brother Kevin took out the special present he had received that year—a tape recorder. For us kids, it was about the coolest thing we'd ever seen, since we almost never got expensive gifts for Christmas, especially something electronic. It was a reel-to-reel style with a flip switch to record, rewind or play. We all assumed Ma and Dad had given it to Kevin because he was about to go into the Army. I learned some years later that he had bought it with money he'd earned and given it to Ma and Dad to give to him for Christmas.

When you're one of twelve kids, you're always battling to get your voice heard. A tape recorder was like a magic stage. Whatever you had to say, no matter how silly or ridiculous, the rest of the family stopped what they were doing and listened while it was recorded. Then we would all listen to it again as it was played back. Not only would we all listen, we would all laugh and talk about it afterwards too.

So, there we were in a crowded apartment Christmas night—an over-sized family with a penchant for singing and a tape recorder. It was like lighting a match in a tinderbox. And who was responsible for the spark that ignited a family Christmas tradition? That would be me. Yup, I confess. It was my cute, loud, two-and-a-half year old voice trying to sing the *Twelve Days of Christmas* on Kevin's tape recorder that started it all.

You see, Kevin had decided to interview the younger kids to capture some of their funny malapropisms to play back later for the amusement of the adults. He was trying to imitate Art Linkletter, who had hosted a television show a few years earlier with a segment called *Kids Say the Darndest Things*, which later became a television show hosted by Bill Cosby.

Anyway, Kevin had just finished interviewing Danny, the next youngest to me, and was about to play it back for everybody. I was sitting on my sister Debbie's lap as she tried to teach me how to sing *The Twelve Days of Christmas*. Before Kevin could start playing Danny's interview, I jumped down from Debbie's lap, ran over to the kitchen table, and scrambled up on the chair next to him.

"I wanna say sumpin! I wanna sing into da tape racorder!" I said excitedly.

"And we'd love to hear you," Kevin replied, laughing. "What song do you want to sing?"

"I wanna sing *The Twelb Days till Chrishmas*," I announced.

"*The Twelve Days of Christmas*?" Kevin repeated to make sure.

"That's whad I said!" I replied. "But I don't think I know all da words."

"Okay, you start, and I'll help if you get stuck," Kevin said, trying to hide a smile as he switched on the tape recorder.

"Okay, let's go," I declared, taking a deep breath. Then I belted out, "On da first day till Chrishmas, fibe goldun wings!"

There was a momentary pause and then everyone burst into laughter, followed by loud clapping. I wasn't quite sure what to make of the response, but Kevin smiled at me and told me my singing was great.

The kitchen was now packed. The laughter and applause had brought everyone—eighteen kids and adults—into the room to crowd around the table and listen to my performance. Kevin rewound the tape and played the recording of my abbreviated song. I don't remember how I sounded, but Ma still tells me I sounded like Shirley Temple. My brothers and sisters, however, claim I was closer to one of the gang from *The Little Rascals*. Either way, my recorded performance produced another round of laughter.

Kevin decided if it was this funny the first time, it would be even funnier the second time, especially if he helped me remember verses two through four. As he recorded both my singing and his coaching, he messed up and didn't remember verse four correctly, which created an even more hysterical recording. That opened the flood gates, and everybody rushed to contribute to the singing, if only to be recorded for comical posterity.

After a lot of talking, singing, and shouting, Kevin, Janie, Debbie, and Sean decided to join me in singing all twelve verses of the song. I'm told we got to verse eight before it broke down into a recording of, "Wait, that's not right ..." and, "Hold on, I know how it goes ..." and, "No, we already sang that verse."

We needed help, and when you wanted to know the lyrics to a Christmas song, the two people you went to were Billy and Bobby. They were the experts. So they were brought in to help guide the five of us through the song. We completed the recording, but it was about as smooth and pleasing as rush-hour traffic on a Friday afternoon in Boston.

Billy and Bobby decided to write down the verses to make it easier for us to sing without their coaching. Debbie ran to her room and grabbed a notebook and pencil. While the lyrics were being transcribed, Cathy chimed in that instead of a few people singing the entire song, each sibling should get one verse. Then we could record it as a family song. Sean and Danny immediately raised their hands to claim the fifth verse—*Five Golden Rings*. Gale interjected and suggested that we should all sing the fifth verse together in honor of Stacy.

I asked who Stacy was, and Bobby answered, "She's your older sister, but she went to heaven before you were born."

Then I said, "I miss her. We should sing loud so Shtacy can hear us in heaven."

We all agreed to sing the fifth verse like a refrain and loud enough for Stacy to enjoy it. That would make it work out perfectly—eleven Cunningham kids and eleven verses. Lynn suggested that the verses be assigned according to the age of the sibling, but that was shot down by everyone who didn't want to be a *Milking Maid*, a *French Hen*, or some other odious gift.

After a long haggling session, we finally agreed on everyone's part. Gale and Cathy were allowed to include their husbands and children with them. Now we were all set. All we needed were decent voices and it could be something worth recording. But what we lacked in musical ability, we more than made up for with enthusiasm.

The first run through was pretty hilarious, with everyone doing his or her best serious or comical vocal performance. There were operetta voices, baritones, John Wayne imitations, a Nixon reprisal, and even an attempt at Alvin the Chipmunk. With each successive rendition, the performances became more outrageous. Eventually, we started to improvise the lyrics. Kevin sang, "*Eight brand new hockey sticks*," while Janie added, "*Four Lee Majors posters*." Lee Majors was her new favorite actor at the time. And every performance would finish with me belting out my loudest *Partridge in a Pear Tree* verse. Since I was the youngest and had started this musical fiasco, I was given the honor of singing the first verse.

Although Dad didn't have a verse of his own, he would chime in for the *Five Golden Rings* refrain and sometimes join me for the finale. Ma never joined in the singing. She just smiled and laughed, clearly proud of her musically accomplished children, like one of those parents in *The Music Man*.

After each performance, we would listen to the replay and laugh hysterically while we debated whether or not it was better than the previous version. If it was, we kept it and erased the earlier one. If it wasn't, we recorded the next performance over it. After about a dozen renditions, everyone was beginning to get worn out with the singing and side-splitting laughter. So we had a vote to decide which of the final two versions we liked the most. Kevin erased the other one and then, ala Lawrence Welk, recorded an introduction to *The Cunningham Family Singing The Twelve Days of Christmas*.

We listened to it one final time. Then, like a tired but content rock band after finishing its first album, we sat around joking about our performances and what we would do next Christmas to make them even better.

Everyone agreed that the recording was now a family heirloom and had to be saved. Since it was Kevin's tape recorder, he was charged with the recording's preservation. Of course, like all other Cunningham heirlooms, it was never saved. Kevin left for the Army, and we moved to another apartment in another city, Beverly, the following spring. I'm told that some of us kids supposedly got to Kevin's tape recorder and unknowingly recorded over it, but it could have been Dad too, since he liked to play around with it when he got drunk.

When Christmas rolled around the next year and we realized the recording was lost, we tried a couple of times to make a new version. But the tape recorder was pretty beaten up by then and barely workable. Also, everyone wasn't there at the same time to do the singing. Gale visited at a different time from Cathy, and Lynn had started dating, so she was in and out of the house. Kevin came home on leave but wasn't around much either. It seemed like a promising family tradition had been cut down before it could get enough traction to last.

Still, every year, those who were there would talk about how much fun that one Christmas had been, reliving our performances and promising to recreate them at some point in the future. I would always insist that if we did reprise our performances, I had to sing the first verse. After all, I was the youngest in the family and the one who actually started the whole tradition.

With every new Christmas, we talked about the recording a little less. After three years in the service, Kevin returned home, got married, and started his own family. Lynn moved out to an apartment and then got married as well. Billy and Bobby went off to college, and Debbie got married and had a child. Although everybody would stop by during the holidays, it was never on the same day or at the same time. Everyone was at a different point in life, and full family gatherings at Christmas were no more.

Then it happened—Christmas night, 1985. Gale, Cathy, Kevin, and Debbie were all visiting with their families. Billy and Bobby took the train up from Boston where they were living, and Lynn showed up with her family for a surprise visit. The other four of us—Janie, Sean, Danny, and me—were still living at home. For the first time in eleven years, all of the Cunninghams were together for Christmas. Including spouses and children, there were now twenty-seven loud and boisterous people celebrating on Christmas night in another not-so-large, smoky, three-bedroom apartment, this time in Beverly. It was great!

Everyone got to talking again about that one Christmas when we taped our rendition of *The Twelve Days of Christmas*. We all jokingly agreed that Kevin owed everybody royalties for not preserving that recording. Obviously, it would have been on *Billboard's Top Ten Christmas Songs* all these years had it been saved. Fortunes could have been made! We had almost as much fun reminiscing about that recording session as we did the actual event itself. At the age of thirteen, I was old enough now to truly appreciate how special that Christmas night had been back in 1974, even if I didn't remember much of it.

And of course, with all of the siblings together on Christmas night, it was bound to happen again. Who needed the original? We would just record another version. Someone clearly wanted us to because it just so happened that Janie got a cassette player for Christmas that year that could also record. And she had a blank cassette just waiting to be used. We had the technology, we had the song, and we had the voices! Okay, two out of three ain't bad.

But no one could remember who had sung which verse back then. That's when Billy took out the original, hand-written copy of the lyrics with notations on it of who had sung what. He had saved it from our original recording session! It was old and faded and looked like one of the *Dead Sea Scrolls*, but it was just legible enough to make out who had which verse. I, of course, had the first one.

How Billy had the foresight to bring the lyrics that night, I don't know, but we were all happy he did. I guess when you grow up poor, without a lot of Christmas presents, happy family celebrations, or basic stability, you want to save everything you can from those special moments because they're as rare and valuable as any present you get. And they last forever.

With everybody assigned a verse, there was nothing left to do but sing. And sing we did! It was just as much fun as the first time, or what I remembered of it. In some ways, I think it was even better because so many new family members—spouses and nieces and nephews—got to experience it as well. Also, I was older, so I could appreciate the event from a grown-up point of view, as well as enjoy the little kids experiencing it for the first time. The tradition was now bigger and, hopefully, would last even longer. We performed eight or nine takes, finally settling on the best version.

This time, Janie was entrusted to keep the recording for Christmas posterity, or until next Christmas when we would try to perform an even better version. Of course, when the next Christmas rolled around and everyone wanted to listen to it, the cassette was nowhere to be found. We had moved again, to another apartment in Beverly, and it was lost. It was a shame, but the tradition had been resurrected and would never disappear.

Many years have since passed, and we still haven't gotten all of the siblings together again at the same time for Christmas. But it doesn't matter, because remembering those Christmases has become a tradition in the best sense. Every member of the Cunningham family—siblings, spouses, nieces, and nephews—no matter where they are, enjoy reminiscing about those stories. Whoever gets together on Christmas will joke around about the song and our family singing tradition.

Sometimes, they even try to do their own version. Other times, they just tell the stories. All of the time, though, they celebrate family.

I know this all sounds kind of corny, but it's really not. Nobody goes through the stuff we did growing up and comes out unscathed, thinking the world is just one carefree bundle of joy with a few tough times to make you appreciate it. Life for all of us was too often painful and cruel. But we were resilient and somehow survived the bad times and the worst times.

I think it was probably our sense of family that got us through. That's what this tradition of singing at Christmas is really all about. It's a special gift that we give to each other every year, and although it doesn't cost anything, the experience of singing *The Twelve Children of Christmas* together is truly priceless.

That's what was going through my mind as I sat on the floor of Billy's living room with my two-month old daughter on my lap wondering what I was going to write for this collection. It was Billy's annual Christmas party that he and his wife Patty threw for friends and family. Every year, he would wrap up the party with a Christmas caroling sing-along. The last song was always *The Twelve Days of Christmas*. Billy would break up the hundred plus guests into twelve groups and assign a different verse to each one. Then everyone would sing, loud and raucous, just like we used to do.

This year, before the singing started, Billy told the story of how *The Twelve Days of Christmas* became a Cunningham family tradition and how his sister Erika started it all. He then pointed to me and welcomed my precious daughter Zoe as the newest family member to take up the tradition. Of course, I insisted on being part of the group who would sing the first verse. The last child of Christmas always sings the first verse. You don't mess with tradition …

Once and Forever

There were twelve of us, the Cunningham kids, together against the world and against the times. But that was long ago.

We've had twenty-four children and nine grandchildren between us since. Dad died almost fifteen years ago, from emphysema, too young. Ma is still alive, amazingly, but she's had to cheat death a few times, kind of like the bill collectors when we were kids. Through some grace, no one else has died.

Some of us have scattered to other parts of the country, maybe to escape, or to not have to remember. But most are still in the Boston area. There have been divorces and second marriages, new crises and scars, and all the problems and disorders you would expect with someone suffering from post-traumatic stress.

At first, no one wanted to remember anything about growing up together, never mind write about it. It was a war, by any measure, and we were just kids. But after *The Twelve Children of Christmas* was finished, something changed, as if a voice had whispered to each of us to try, try to remember. Memories came back, for all of us, some good and some bad and some terrible.

But the Christmas ones were almost all good, and we shared them again, like we had growing up. We shared them with our kids, and for some of us, our grandkids. We remembered what we should never forget—we were a family once, and we will be forever.

www.ingramcontent.com/pod-product-compliance
Lightning Source LLC
Chambersburg PA
CBHW071904090426

42811CB00004B/737